The History of Ancient Israel

BLOOMSBURY GUIDES FOR THE PERPLEXED

Bloomsbury's Guides for the Perplexed are clear, concise and accessible introductions to thinkers, writers and subjects that students and readers can find especially challenging. Concentrating specifically on what it is that makes the subject difficult to grasp, these books explain and explore key themes and ideas, guiding the reader towards a thorough understanding of demanding material.

Guides for the Perplexed available from Bloomsbury include:
Biblical Criticism: A Guide for the Perplexed, Eryl W. Davies
Eschatology in the Bible: A Guide for the Perplexed, Edward Adams
Paul: A Guide for the Perplexed, Timothy G. Gombis
Oral Tradition and the New Testament: A Guide for the Perplexed, Rafael Rodriguez
The New Testament and Jewish Law: A Guide for the Perplexed, James Crossley
The Origin of the Bible: A Guide for the Perplexed, Lee Martin McDonald

Forthcoming Guides for the Perplexed available from Bloomsbury include:
The Bible and Spatial Theory: A Guide for the Perplexed, Christopher Meredith

The History of Ancient Israel

A Guide for the Perplexed

Philip R. Davies

Bloomsbury T&T Clark
An imprint of Bloomsbury Publishing Plc

B L O O M S B U R Y
LONDON • NEW DELHI • NEW YORK • SYDNEY

Bloomsbury T&T Clark

An imprint of Bloomsbury Publishing Plc

Imprint previously known as T&T Clark

50 Bedford Square	1385 Broadway
London	New York
WC1B 3DP	NY 10018
UK	USA

www.bloomsbury.com

BLOOMSBURY, T&T CLARK and the Diana logo are trademarks of Bloomsbury Publishing Plc

First published 2015

© Philip R. Davies, 2015

British Library Cataloguing-in-Publication Data

A catalogue record for this book is available from the British Library.

ISBN: HB: 978-0-56765-584-4
PB: 978-0-56765-585-1
ePDF: 978-0-56765-582-0
ePub: 978-0-56765-583-7

Library of Congress Cataloging-in-Publication Data

A catalogue record for this book is available from the British Library.

Series: Guides for the Perplexed

Typeset by Fakenham Prepress Solutions, Fakenham, Norfolk NR21 8NN
Printed and bound in India

CONTENTS

List of Abbreviations vii
Prologue viii

1 Orientation 1

Part One: History

2 What is History? 17

3 Origins of Ancient Historiography 27

4 Biblical Historiography 39

Part Two: 'Israel'

5 Ancient Israel(s) in the Iron Age 65

6 The 'New Israels': The Post-monarchic Era 79

Part Three: Ancient History and the Social Sciences

7 Archaeology 103

8 Sociological Approaches to History 119

Part Four: Constructing a History of 'Ancient Israel'

9 Synthesizing Data and Approaches 139

10 A Bibliographical Review 153

Notes 167
Bibliography 171
Index of Modern Authors 181
Index of Ancient Sources 184

ABBREVIATIONS

BA   Biblical Archaeologist

BAR   Biblical Archaeology Review

JBL   Journal of Biblical Literature

JHS   Journal of Hebrew Scriptures

JSOT Journal for the Study of the Old Testament

PROLOGUE

Looking both ways

With every book of this kind there is a dilemma: should it introduce primarily the great body of work of the past, the way things stand at present, or the prospects opening up for the future? The reader probably hopes for all three, and this *Guide* aims to achieve a balance between them, though with a little more emphasis on the new agendas looming into view than on to the agendas of previous generations of textbooks. There is another balance to be struck between describing what historians have claimed to discover, what we seem at present to know, and basic questions about what a 'History of Ancient Israel' is. I have minimized the 'history of research' component because of the quite radical changes in the genre of 'History of Ancient Israel' that are taking place as this book is being written. Paradoxically, these changes partly involve going back to basics, starting from the beginning. Hence the first part of the book is driven by the questions 'what is history?' and 'what is (or was) "ancient Israel?"' The second part will deal with how a modern historian might fashion the kind of history that the various methods and data actually allow to be done. So much is being written on this topic in the last few decades that it is quite difficult to convey a clear impression and certainly impossible to acknowledge adequately all the contributions that have been made to a very lively debate. I am painfully aware of many omissions, and can only hope that some readers of this *Guide* will read further and make good these omissions.

A special kind of history?

It's a good idea to begin by stepping back from the subject a little and asking why so much attention should be devoted to this relatively small period and place in human history. For while this chunk of the human past should be of concern to the modern historian as much as any other (the most eloquent, but also edgy, statement of this case being by Whitelam 1996), it never has been, and probably never will be, approached in the same way as, say, the history of ancient China or even of Egypt. The reason is simply that this bit of the past is what has long been called the 'biblical period', and the territory in which it takes place the 'land of the Bible'. Its story has been written up in what became Jewish and Christian scriptures, and is also rehearsed in the Qur'an. The genre of History of Israel has therefore been the domain not of professional historians, but biblical scholars, and the subject has been taught within Theology or Divinity syllabuses. Until late in the last century histories were following the custom of using the biblical story as the template for their own account, including a 'Patriarchal Age' 'Conquest' 'Period of the Judges' and an 'Exile and Restoration'. Bible atlases also depicted geographically correct maps on which biblical places and events were marked, as if these stories were equally objective representations.

Ancient Israel and Judah are a special part of history because they are scriptural, and as such they have become not only ingrained in Jewish and Christian religious worship and teaching but also part of the historical consciousness of the Western world, part of its prehistory. The cultural tradition and religious investment has in the last century been augmented by the historical claims implicit in Zionism and the use of archaeology to undergird these claims. The general resurgence of religious fundamentalism has also helped to sustain the view that Bible is literally history. The political expression of this view has in turn provoked a rejection of the biblical story by Palestinians, even a denial of the existence of any 'ancient Israel'. But the uniqueness of this bit of the past is not merely its status as a sacred history. Even where the historian rightly discounts such a religious status as conferring historical privilege, these writings are nevertheless, products of ancient Palestine, creations of ancient Israelite and Judahite writers, and, as

we can now see in the biblical Dead Sea scrolls from Qumran, they
were concrete historical artefacts with particular historical uses,
meanings and readers. There is no other segment of ancient history
in which such a collection of writings has been preserved. They *do*,
or at least they *can*, tell us a great deal about the times and places
they come from, about their authors and readers and about the
social world in which they were created. Even if they were *entirely*
unreliable in what they narrate (which is not the case), their very
existence reveals something. Even fictions never totally conceal
the real world. In other words, if David did not rule over most of
Palestine (as seems to be the case), then the portrait of this king
and his empire must tell us something of historical value. Why
was this story generated? The historian's duty is not exhausted by
determining the historicity or otherwise of David and his empire:
belief in him and his achievements has to be taken into account,
because it has influenced human behaviour and thus played a role
in making its own history. Christianity itself, in proclaiming a
Messiah, is testifying to the power of the story and reminding us
that it is not simply the real events of the past that determine our
actions but what we believe about the past.

What sort of history?

During the last century, and now with increasing clarity, it has
become obvious that reconstructing the history of the kingdoms
of Israel and Judah, and their successor provinces of Samaria and
Yehud is a matter as much, if not more, for the archaeologist as for
the biblical scholar. Since the beginnings of archaeological research
in the late nineteenth century, the role of survey and excavation
in Palestine has played an ever-increasing role in recreating the
past. Having begun as a means of verifying and illuminating
the Bible, playing a rather subordinate role, it has now not only
become the dominant partner but showing signs of creating its
own independent account. Some archaeologists even claim that it
is for them and not biblical scholars to write this history, and the
claim is supported by the nature of archaeological research itself,
which has matured from the recovery of artefacts for museums
and the uncovering of monumental structures for tourists to gaze

upon to an interdisciplinary and highly technological analysis of all traces of the human past. It has become an explicitly anthropological discipline. After a century in which the reigning question was whether or not archaeology confirmed the Bible, and how the results of each kind of enquiry could be harmonized, it is now apparent that archaeological and biblical histories are ultimately focused on different things. Archaeology offers a new way of writing ancient history, a story of how humans interact with their environment and with each other, how they move, eat, live and die, and organize themselves socially. It is a history of processes, cultures, habits, rather than of individual events. The French historians Marc Bloch and Fernand Braudel and the *Annales* school (see Burke 2013) distinguished between *histoire événementielle*, 'history of events', the short-term timescale dominated by biography and incidents, and the *longue durée*, the long-term processes of evolving structures and patterns of human behaviour. It replaced the study of great individuals with those of the lives of ordinary people and politics, diplomacy, and wars with human (settlement patterns, agriculture, trade, technology, communication) and natural (geography, geology, climate) focusing on social groups and their 'mentalities'. This approach also recognizes the importance of including all levels of society and addressing collective consciousness and purpose rather than that of individuals. Among historians of ancient Palestine, Whitelam (2013) has tried to apply this method, which clearly prioritizes archaeological rather than literary research.

This way of writing history is not, of course, the only one, and it has been challenged, especially in cases where there is an abundance of historical documentation, by those who still wish to affirm that history is made by the actions of extraordinary individuals, a view that the biblical stories of the past uphold. 'Post-processual' archaeology, too, reacting against a too positivistic method of interpreting data, has insisted that archaeology is a human and not a natural science, whose conclusions cannot be free of subjectivity; in the field of ancient Israel and Judah that warning is clearly justified, given the extent of disagreement among archaeologists and the very clear ideological agenda that can sometimes be discerned. On the other hand, what was once called 'historical-critical exegesis', the enterprise of interpreting texts as historical products and not works of literary art, has been learning to expand its repertoire to embrace many kinds of literary-critical approaches, including narratology and ideological criticism. 'New criticism', 'new historicism' and 'mnemohistory', as Jan Assmann (1992) has called the study of ancient collective memory, have all helped to bring studies of the biblical literature into the human sciences and into engagement with the material world of the past.

The prospect for historian of ancient Israel and Judah is thus rather daunting but exciting and the demands quite severe. It is no longer possible for the discipline to serve merely as a component of Theology or Divinity, but neither should it be taught by archaeologists untrained in biblical criticism. To do it justice requires a well-trained historian. All of the main sources of information require interrogation: none can be taken at face value. The biblical stories are the most obviously unreliable, as is evident from comparison with other evidence but also on purely internal analysis. But equally, inscriptions require a 'hermeneutic of suspicion', for they are not created in order to tell future genera-tions the truth of what they record, but to promote the image and achievements of the king ('state ideology'), and in doing so they may invent or distort. The data obtained by archaeology do not deliberately mislead, but by the very randomness of preservation they can encourage misleading interpretation. The history of biblical archaeology shows how easily apparently 'hard' data can be interpreted in a desired direction.

The modern historian thus an interpreter of data – but also a storyteller. We cannot properly speak of '*the* history of ancient Israel'. There can only be 'histories', and even the best critical histories can never be proved accurate, but only shown to be inaccurate wherever evidence or argument makes the case. In this sense histories are rather like scientific hypotheses, but with the very important difference that we cannot go back in time to verify our stories, and in the end we must learn to live with different interpretations.

Key issues in contemporary discussion

In the following chapters, attention will be directed at major features of debate among modern biblical historians. First is the methodological one: what do we mean by 'history' and how do we identify it among our various ways of engaging with the past? Partly, we can understand or modern 'historical consciousness' by reflecting on ancient discourse, including biblical historiography (if that is an appropriate term). Such methodological reflection is a relatively recent phenomenon among historians of ancient Israel and Judah but in part it reflects a wider interest in method, ideology and presupposition within biblical studies generally.

The second major issue is the label 'Israel'. It has become apparent that the biblical narratives do not in fact use the name in a single straightforward way. What is the relationship between an ancient kingdom that certainly bore the name 'Israel', a people consisting of twelve tribes that included both the population of the kingdom of Israel and the population of Judah, and an 'Israel' that consists only of Judah – namely, the 'Israel' that is also-called 'Judaism'? Is the term primarily ethnic, or political, or religious? Of which Israel(s), if not all, will the historian write, and how will the relationship between them be explained?

Having explained the problems with both 'history' and 'ancient Israel' we shall turn to the various disciplinary resources at the historian's disposal: archaeology, anthropology, sociology and some literary-critical approaches, looking especially at how it is possible to integrate them into a single historical reconstruction.

Finally, this *Guide* offers a brief review of some useful resources from recent history writing and a survey of a selection of histories that illustrate the range of approaches that are currently on offer. It is hoped that at this point readers will have gained enough understanding to make up their own minds as to the relative virtues and defects of these various ways of reconstructing what we now have to call 'ancient Israels'.

1

Orientation

Retrospect

In the last fifty years, the study of ancient Israel's history has changed quite dramatically. It will be helpful at the beginning of this *Guide* to explain the background to these changes and set out broadly the agenda(s) directing current investigation of ancient Israelite history.

The most fundamental shift to have occurred in the last fifty years is the relationship between the texts of the Hebrew Bible/Old Testament, which include extensive narratives about Israel, and the evidence available at an ever more rapid rate from archaeological excavation and survey. In both areas there have been significant advances: on the one side an increasing range of insights and techniques applied to historical-critical biblical exegesis, and on the other technological and theoretical developments that enable greater sophistication in the analysis and interpretation of archaeological data. In each case there have been quite dramatic developments in the historical outlines with which scholars are currently working.

Until the advent of scientific Middle Eastern archaeology around the beginning of the twentieth century, the major scholarly arguments over 'biblical history' had engaged only with the biblical texts, which were traditionally accepted by most people as a definitive account of not only the people of Israel and their past, but even as an account of the creation of the world (and a prediction of its end). Yet while the evidence of the natural sciences led to an enormous controversy over the biblical stories of creation in the second half of the nineteenth century, critical arguments had been developing earlier against the reliability of the Bible as a historical source. Already in the seventeenth century Spinoza had argued that the books of Moses (Genesis to Deuteronomy) had not been written by him, as traditionally maintained, but assembled over a period of time, from various sources. Various other thinkers, influenced by the Enlightenment belief in rationality and in a denial of divine revelation through scriptures (among the best known being Voltaire and Thomas Payne) derided the Bible as an authoritative historical source. But such outright scepticism left an unsatisfactory choice: myth or history? Scholarship needed to find a way between these alternatives that engaged critically with historical knowledge.

In fact, it proved possible to write a critical history that used the Bible. The culmination of this enterprise, using what is generally referred to as 'literary-historical criticism' was represented by the 'New Documentary Hypothesis' elaborated by Julius Wellhausen (1844–1918) in 1885, but based on the work of several others, notably W. M. L. de Wette (1780–1849) and Karl Heinrich Graf (1815–69). This hypothesis focused on the first five or six books of the Hebrew Bible, that is, the Pentateuch or the Hexateuch, and remained a basis for historical-critical biblical scholarship well into the twentieth century. Its main contention is that these books can be assigned to a combination of four documents, and that these documents can be provided with a chronological sequence (J[ahwist], E[lohist], D[euteronomy], P[riestly], in that order); and these in turn formed the basis for a reconstruction of the development of the religion of 'ancient Israel'.

The foundation of such a historical reconstruction is the conclusion that the lawgiving by Moses did not stand at, or near, the beginning of Israelite religion, but marked a later, 'postexilic' (fifth century BCE) transition to Judaism. The stories in the books of Judges and Samuel, for example, did not, as de Wette and, later, Wellhausen pointed out, presuppose that the laws of Moses were acknowledged and practised by Israelites. It is important to note that this literary-historical project addressed largely the history of 'Israelite religion' and not political or social history or ethnography. The biblical sources taken on their own were after all not easily interrogated on such matters. Wellhausen concluded that Israel's early religion was characterized by the ethical teaching of the

prophets, and he thus depicted a rather negative decline into legalistic and ritual religion that in his view characterized Judaism. If
this evaluation has now been abandoned, other important elements
of this reconstruction still stand, though in many ways historical
research has qualified and redefined Wellhausen's reconstruction
of the course of 'Israelite religion' and the early development of
Judaism. A new form of religion does seem to have emerged in the
fifth century in both Judah and Samaria, and probably more widely
in Syria-Palestine, but our understanding of early forms of Judaism
reveals, far from a monolithic and ritually obsessed religious
system, an enormous variety and vigour of beliefs and practice. The
notion of a 'prophetic religion' has also dissipated, and 'pre-exilic'
Israelite religious beliefs now appear to have been hardly different
from the pattern in the rest of Palestine. Nevertheless, Wellhausen
was quite conscious of the fact that since, as de Wette had put it,
and he underlined, texts tell us about the time they are written
and not (necessarily) the time they claim to describe, and since
he dated Deuteronomy and the Priestly 'documents' to well after
the foundation of the monarchies, he cast doubt on the entire
reliability of the Pentateuchal narratives. But he did not extend this
doubt to the narratives of Joshua–Kings, which were, in part, taken
to show precisely that the Mosaic laws were not in force at the time
they describe. His hypothesis, then, depended on these books being
accepted as a fairly accurate historical account.

Some of the revisions to this reconstruction have been due to
increased attention to the biblical texts themselves, but study of
early Jewish texts outside the scriptural canon, the 'Apocrypha
and Pseudepigrapha' as they are commonly termed, as well as the
Dead Sea scrolls, discovered in 1947, have cast doubt on just how
representative a portrait the Bible gives of Israelite and Jewish
religion. But the contribution of archaeology in Palestine and
elsewhere in the Middle East has also changed the way Israelite –
in fact, we shall now have to say 'Israelite and Judean' – history
now has to be investigated. Even before scientific excavation
began to be conducted, inscriptions from neighbouring countries
(Egypt, Assyria, Babylonia, Iran Syria, Moab) had begun to
throw direct light on persons and events in the Bible. While these
texts are usually discovered by means of archaeology, they are
still literary texts, and cannot be treated as 'objective' testimony.
Like the biblical narratives, and indeed like all ancient texts, they

represent certain interests and ideologies. They can indeed provide verification of some events and personages, but there is always a perspective, a motive, and indeed, sometimes the demands of the literary genre, underlying an account of even a contemporary event. Indeed, it is not incorrect to regard all ancient texts, the production of which was largely under the control of monarchs and their servants, as propagandistic and thus not to be interpreted too naively. Here literary-critical rather than archaeological skills are needed by the historian.

Nowadays, archaeological survey and excavation, and the scientific analysis of artefacts, is increasingly recognized as a primary means of reconstructing ancient Palestinian history. How this corpus of knowledge should stand alongside the biblical narratives, how the two kinds of material should be combined by the historian, has provided the major theme of scholarly debate for a century. 'Biblical archaeology', as it was once called, came into existence with a religious, specifically Christian, agenda. Its pioneers were sponsored by organizations created to explore the Levant for material evidence of 'biblical history', to bring the biblical world into material existence – and, implicitly, to undermine the kind of critical historical reconstruction mentioned above which seemed to relegate much of the biblical narrative, at least relating to the origins of 'Israel', to the category of wishful thinking or wilful creation. The goal of these archaeologists was to counter such reconstruction, illustrating the historical reality of the biblical story by recovery of its material remains. For more than half of the twentieth century, a struggle took place, not between Bible and archaeology – which were assumed to be mutually confirmatory – but between this combination of Bible *plus* 'biblical archaeology', and biblical criticism, which also attempted to use the results of archaeology, but in order to refine its own reconstruction of the past and its understanding of the biblical texts. Numerous semi-scholarly works in the twentieth century also proclaimed that archaeology had 'proved the Bible right'. But any search of the internet today will indeed find that according to the majority of sites, the Bible is historically true and that archaeology proves it. Neither statement is true, however much some wish it to be. Scholarly and popular views of the history of 'ancient Israel' are still strongly divergent.

The hottest debate between the two approaches concerned those cases where literary-historical criticism shed doubt and where archaeology might offer illumination. The Exodus, though a central episode of biblical history, has never been amenable to plausible archaeological confirmation (there are similar Egyptian accounts of such an episode in the early history of the Judeans, but these date from the fourth century BCE; see Chapter 9). Debate centred, for the most part, on the so-called 'patriarchal age' and the lifestyle of Abraham, Isaac and Jacob, as reflected, so the arguments went, in ancient Near Eastern texts; and on the Israelite 'conquest' of Canaan, as apparently evidenced by the destruction of a number of cities, most dramatically Hazor. The most influential exponent of 'biblical archaeology' was the American William F. Albright, and the best-known history book to emerge from his circle is that of John Bright (1960). Later editions of this popular book nevertheless reflect Bright's shift away from some of Albright's conclusions. Albright himself wrote an ambitious book called *From the Stone Age to Christianity* (1942), which deserves attention because it illustrates how, particularly in the United States, biblical history, and especially religion, is seen by many as part of a divinely directed world history leading from Israel to Western civilization, and pre-eminently to the United States. For Albright, as for many others, ancient Israelite history was part of his own and his nation's prehistory. And if this perception is exaggerated, it is not without some insight. Why *are* we interested in the history of ancient Israel, if not because in Christian culture this biblical story has been embedded in the collective religious consciousness?

Historians who rejected the approach of 'biblical archaeology' and persisted with literary-historical criticism attempted to interpret the results of archaeology in line with their own understanding of the biblical texts. This approach is especially associated with Albrecht Alt in Germany, and represented by the history book written by his student Martin Noth (1958). The approach here was to treat the biblical narrative as representing what ancient Israelites believed or remembered of their past, their 'traditions'; and they attempted to reconstruct a history of these traditions. How did these 'traditions' relate to the documents that Wellhausen and others had identified in an earlier phase of literary-historical criticism? In his *History of Pentateuchal Traditions* (1948, ET 1972), Noth seemed to suggest another direction by dividing the 'tradition' into themes – guidance out of Egypt, guidance into the arable land, promise to the patriarchs, guidance in the wilderness and 'revelation at Sinai', which were originally unrelated to each other but came to be gathered together to form the basis of the Pentateuchal story in a quite early composition. Of this story, Noth claimed that it could not be considered by the historian as a history or even a prehistory of Israel, but as materials drawn from the prehistory of Israelite tribes. The history of Israel properly began, in his view, when these tribes came together into a league, an 'amphictyony', after their settlement in Canaan. This was, in his view, how Israel was first formed. But Noth still believed in the Pentateuchal sources, which he thought were developed as different versions of this combined tradition. Later, it was proposed (Rendtorff 1990) that the theory of an early source unifying these themes, later elaborated into the Pentateuchal source-documents theory was unnecessary: the Pentateuch could have begun with the themes, which were later combined into a single narrative – a more economical explanation.

For Noth, as for Alt, there had been no 'conquest' of the kind related in the book of Joshua, but something closer to the portrait of the book of Judges where individual tribes settled individually but acted cooperatively. The story of the miraculous destruction of Jericho, therefore, drew on details of a celebration of land possession in the form of a ritual procession around the ruins, and the story of the conquest of Ai was generated by the presence of a conspicuous ruin. Here we can see the first attempt to give a rational historical explanation of stories that were unhistorical, a task that has now become central to the whole enterprise of 'ancient Israelite history', especially under the general approach of 'cultural memory' (see Chapter 8), which replaces the earlier notion of 'tradition'. Noth followed Alt's suggestion that the Israelites came into Canaan through largely peaceful infiltration, gradually changing from nomadic or seminomadic lifestyles to a settled, agricultural one. The tribes that were to form Israel entered from outside, but in a piecemeal process in which seasonal movement in and out of the arable land gave way to permanent occupation of largely deserted areas. As will be seen, this suggestion was to be partly confirmed by archaeological survey in the 1970s.

Noth's contemporary, Gerhard von Rad, was also a tradition-historian, but his interests were substantially theological and not historical. His suggestion was that the Pentateuchal story grew from a short basic creed, whose original form could still be found in Deut. 26.5–10:

> A wandering Aramean was my ancestor; he went down into Egypt and lived there as an alien, few in number, and there he became a great nation, mighty and populous. When the Egyptians treated us harshly and afflicted us, by imposing hard labour on us, we cried to Yahweh, the god of our ancestors; Yahweh heard our voice and saw our affliction, our toil, and our oppression. Yahweh brought us out of Egypt with a mighty hand and an outstretched arm, with a terrifying display of power, and with signs and wonders.

What is missing here is the lawgiving at Sinai, which, von Rad argued, was not part of the earliest tradition. In this he was able to affirm the older historical-critical view that the Mosaic Law was no part of early Israel's religion. Von Rad also made the point, perhaps better than Noth, that the method of Albright and his students, which led to what was known as the 'biblical theology movement' (articulated especially by G. Ernest Wright, 1960; see von Rad 1961 for a rejoinder) prioritized the historical events as the basis of religious belief, valuing the biblical story as a testimony to the demonstration of the divine purpose in history, was theologically dangerous. It meant that any biblical texts proving to be unhistorical were left without a function and devoid of religious value. But on the contrary, as Christian scripture, it is the biblical tradition, and not the facts behind it, that should possess authority for the believer.

Here is an interesting paradox: the Albright school and the 'biblical theology movement' were not necessarily committed to any *religious* view of the Bible's historicity. Insofar as its accounts were inspired or authoritative, they were so by virtue of their testimony to the divine purpose. The tradition-historians, however, and especially von Rad, accepted that the biblical story of Israel was scriptural and as such had to be valued as a testimony to the religious faith that defined Israel itself. Israel's beliefs about its election by the true god were the point, and not the accuracy of its historical memory. The notion that stories define group identity, as just mentioned, plays an important role in contemporary historical research, moving the focus away from the search for verification of historical details in the stories.

For the historian does have to try to understand and evaluate biblical texts and stories that are judged unhistorical. They cannot be discarded, because these stories, and the texts that contain them, are still products of history: at some time someone wrote them, and for reasons that we are surely obliged to try and find out. Hence 'tradition-history', even where it concludes that traditions cannot be claimed as narrating history, is still investigating history: the history of beliefs about the past and the history of producing texts about the past. We might say that the production of the Bible is part of the social history of 'ancient Israel' – or rather, of more than one ancient Israel. This principle is essentially what Wellhausen himself recognized (and biblical archaeologists forgot): that texts tell us about the time they were written, rather than the time about which they seem to be writing. This principle increasingly informs the work of the modern historian of 'ancient Israel'.

Let us now continue our review of history writing in the twentieth century. If there existed a basic disagreement over the status of the stories in Genesis to Joshua, this did not extend to the period after the settlement in Canaan. Only one major difference between Bright and Noth, the most influential mid-twentieth-century historians, on whose work more than one generation of scholars was reared, strikes the reader in the historical reconstructions of either approach. It does not seem a contentious one, but in hindsight it is significant. Bright's *History* ends with the re-purification of the temple by Judas Maccabee in the second century BCE, followed by a short chapter on early Judaism; Noth continues to the revolt of the Jews under bar Kosiba (bar Cochba) in the second century CE. Thus, one story ends on a joyous note, the other on a dismal one, with the words 'thus ended the ghastly epilogue of Israel's history'. This contrast actually sounds a curious echo of the two biblical historiographies, for while the books of Kings end with Judahites and their king exiled in Babylon, Chronicles ends with the decree of Cyrus allowing Judahites to return (and it is surely for this reason that Chronicles occupies its odd place at the end of the Hebrew canon). From this difference we can learn that writing a history of 'ancient Israel' entails judgements about endings and beginnings. Where does 'ancient Israel' stop? This depends on what the historian chooses to define as 'Israel' (this is addressed in Chapters 5 and 6).

But since Bright and Noth wrote, the focus of debate has moved on from the contents of the Pentateuch (essentially the nineteenth-century arena) and the patriarchs, exodus, conquest and settlement (the twentieth-century arena) to the monarchic and post-monarchic eras. The conflicts between the biblical narrative and the findings of archaeology now range across the events featuring Saul, David, Solomon and, later, Ezra and Nehemiah. The post-monarchic era, in which the provinces of Judah and Israel/Samaria continued their history of contentious neighbourliness, has also become disputed territory. Abraham and Moses were already questionable figures among the literary-historical critics: now David, the 'united monarchy' and the great empire stretching from Egypt to the Euphrates are being questioned. The 'Exile' also, and its sequel, the 'Restoration' have been subject to reassessment, and here we are now arguing still about the origins of an 'ancient Israel' but in the guise of what will become 'Judaism', whatever that is and whatever its relationship to earlier religious systems. There is, in fact, hardly any period of the history covered by the biblical narratives that is not under quite intense (and sometimes rather ill-tempered) critical review.

Recent developments

So where is the 'history of ancient Israel' at present? In the last forty years a revolution has taken place, which has (at least in the view of most biblical historians) reconfigured the relationship between the biblical narratives and archaeology and required a new approach to biblical historiographical narrative.

It is therefore ironical that the final collapse of 'biblical archaeology' with its broad verification of the biblical story came about not through the arguments of literary-historical critics – though these made a considerable contribution – but following a survey of ancient sites in the newly occupied West Bank (which constitutes the home of most of ancient Israel and Judah) by Israeli archaeologists. The revolution was sudden: during the 1970s the combined efforts of biblical critics and archaeological surveys set a new agenda for historical research, the ramifications of which are far-reaching and have probably not even yet been fully grasped.

During this decade biblical historians, integrating archaeological data with the biblical texts, also dismantled two of the pillars of 'biblical archaeology'. First, the thesis of a historical 'patriarchal' or 'ancestral' period' – to which Abraham, Isaac and Jacob and their families could be assigned – was disposed of in two almost simultaneous books by Thomas Thompson (1974) and John Van Seters (1975), who showed that evidence from either archaeology or ancient non-biblical texts claimed to illuminate these individuals, or their customs and lifestyle did not add up. Shortly afterwards. The other pillar, the Israelite 'conquest' of Canaan – by now in any case becoming more and more qualified – was replaced by Norman Gottwald (1979). Developing an idea proposed by George Mendenhall in 1962, Gottwald argued that Israel came into being as a group of Canaanite farmers (peasants) who withdrew from the dominant political system and established a new egalitarian society in the highlands. This thesis went beyond earlier models of the Israelite 'settlement' as a process of infiltration into largely unoccupied territory that had been proposed by Alt and his followers. For although he accepted the existence of an 'Exodus group' among this population, Gottwald understood 'Israel' to have been composed of Canaanites in what was popularly referred to as a 'peasants' revolt'.

In Gottwald's reconstruction we can also see what might be called a third discipline that has come to play an important role in reconstructing ancient Israelite and Judahite history. While in the United States archaeology is generally taught and studied within anthropology, in many places (including Great Britain) it is a separate discipline. In either case, anthropology is a science with many branches, the most relevant of which is what in Great Britain is called 'social anthropology' and in the USA 'cultural anthropology'. It is basically the study of social systems, though the variety of methods and approaches used worldwide make it difficult to describe succinctly. Of particular importance is the comparative approach to human social behaviour, in which contemporary 'pre-industrial' societies can be observed and analysed as a mean of understanding societies in the past that no longer exist. Such comparative studies also assist in the formulation of general rules about human social behaviour that can be appealed to in the analysis of ancient societies, though the universality and validity of such rules is not everywhere endorsed, and must not be taken rigidly. Human behaviour is not entirely predictable, and we never know all the factors anyway. A better concept than a 'rule' is a 'model' which (like Max Weber's famous 'ideal type') does not dictate how certain processes and behaviours must be, but suggests a set of elements to which they will tend to conform. Nevertheless, modern archaeological work regularly engages in anthropological analysis as a means of interpreting material data. Such a perspective has also been used, for example, in interpreting the development of monarchy in ancient Israel and Judah, or the psychology and social mechanisms typically used by deported populations to preserve elements of their former identity. It would be a poor modern history of ancient Israel and Judah that did not take social/cultural anthropology into account as an aid in description, analysis and explanation of events. It goes without saying that the biblical narratives rarely offer any such explanations.

The priority now given to archaeological data – which have increasingly been interpreted to provide evidence of social habits, belief systems and lifestyles – is bringing about a change also in the historian's approach to biblical texts. If it is true that even in the twentieth-century theological concerns and religious agendas (including Zionism for this purpose) dominated history writing, the proper context has now shifted. No history of ancient Israel can ignore social-scientific frameworks and methodologies. As a result of this shift, historians of ancient Israel and Judah can finally see themselves as behaving in much the same way as all other historians, dissolving the barrier that separated 'sacred history' from 'profane history'.

We should now return to the catalyst of the new order. The new direction just described was prompted above all else by the publication of an archaeological survey undertaken under the direction of Tel Aviv University, beginning in the 1970s. Israel's invasion and occupation of the West Bank in 1967 provided an opportunity to survey and to begin to excavate the all-important central hill country where the kingdoms of Israel and Judah had been centred. These surveys revealed the sudden arrival, at the beginning of the Iron Age (c. 1250 BCE), of farming villages in the central northern highlands and, later, in the highlands of Judah further south. The material culture of these villages exhibited no non-indigenous features and the conclusions initially drawn (and not subsequently recanted) were that these farmers ('farmers' is widely preferred to

'peasants' as less condescending) were drawn from local populations. Where this population came from is still debated. The two
main alternatives are that they were nomadic or seminomadic,
perhaps from the other side of the Jordan, or that they came from
the cities that were suffering economic decline. These alternatives
are not mutually exclusive. It was accepted that this population
group was the only one that could plausibly be identified either
as 'Israel' or as what would become Israel, a 'proto-Israel'. And
so it follows from these conclusions that the Exodus, lawgiving at
Sinai, wilderness wandering and conquest not only cannot have
occurred, but cannot even have formed an early national tradition,
as Martin Noth had maintained. The entire agenda of relating
these stories to actual events in the past now had to be reconceived:
both archaeology and historical-critical exegesis had to move in
new directions. Of particular significance for these directions was
the observation that the hill country had been settled in two phases:
first the northern sector, where the kingdom of Israel was to be
established, and later the Judean highlands. Further work was to
conclude that these areas subsequently developed at different rates
and perhaps independently, with no evidence that they constituted
a single society before becoming separate kingdoms.

What these conclusions entail is on the one hand an accumulation of one kind of historical knowledge but also, in a sense, a
great loss of a different kind of knowledge. The lost 'knowledge' is
the biblical story, which can no longer be relied upon as a secure
framework for any kind of history. Baruch Halpern (1995) referred
to this, dramatically but rather carelessly, as 'erasing history'. But
the stories historian should not overlook the evidence of what
people in the past believed about their own past, even if it was
misguided. These stories still belong to history: they were told,
heard and written in history, and their meanings relate to the
historical contexts in which this process took place. This process is
what the term 'tradition-history' means, and what is now coming
to be investigated under the rubric of 'cultural memory'. Memories
form part of the real history of human societies, ancient as well as
modern. But it is different from a history confined to the recording
and reconstruction of external events.

Prospects

The changes described in the last section are not only quite radical in themselves, but seem to be leading to an even more radical reorientation. We can no longer simply discuss 'what really happened' in the history of 'ancient Israel'. We are now aware that we need to consider what we mean by a 'history' and what we count as 'Israel'. The competent 'biblical historian' (the term itself is a useful shorthand but rather misleading) requires familiarity with not just the results, but the techniques and principles of archaeology, as well as with a range of literary-critical methods and a good grasp of a range of social-scientific theory. In addition, the historian needs to be aware that history is not an objective arbiter of the past. There are no innocent histories, and no historian can satisfy the numerous interests vested in any stories about the past, especially written ones. In what has become a multicultural and even postcolonial world, in which the past is a matter of contested ownership, it is not possible for historical and religious ideas of 'truth' to be equated. Palestine's past is not the property of Christianity, nor even Judaism, nor the state of Israel, nor the Palestinians. Each constituency has its own story to tell, and while the historian can adjudicate to some extent, it is not possible to offer a 'true' history.

For one of the important features of recent scholarship on the history of ancient Israel has been an awareness of philosophical and methodological issues. The 'Bible as history' slogan and the simplistic use of the Bible in 'biblical archaeology' operated without any reflection on what kind of writing about the past we mean by using the word, and in what sense, if at all, we might recognize our definition of 'history' in the biblical stories. The following chapters, then, will be devoted to clarifying what we mean by 'history', identifying the emergence of a consciousness of 'history' itself as we understand it and trying to understand the ways in which the biblical stories of the past represent and understand what it is that occurred beyond the horizon of their actual knowledge. One of the key conclusions to emerge from this study will be that all these historiographies are concerned with establishing their various definitions of 'Israel', and to these we can add the definitions that emerge from ancient inscriptions and from archaeological investigation. We shall then see that the modern historian is confronted not with an 'ancient Israel', but with several. Which of these should we write about: should it not be all of them? The future for the historian of 'ancient Israel(s)' is challenging but also more exciting than perhaps it has ever been.

PART ONE

History

2

What is History?

The next two chapters are not intended merely as a prelude to getting on with the 'real business' of describing what happened in the past, but because they will determine what the 'real business' is. Equally, asking what we mean by 'ancient Israel' will lead to some quite radical, but also logical, redefinitions of what a modern *History of Ancient Israel* ought to be. If 'history' and 'ancient Israel' seem to you straightforward concepts, read these chapters carefully![1]

'History' and 'the past'

In common speech, we often use 'history' to mean 'the past'. But 'history' implies something both more and also less than this. The 'past' includes everything that has been before us, and will always be almost entirely unknown. If we did know it, it would appear to us chaotic, meaningless and mostly of no interest. But this verdict applies to even the sum total of what we *do* know. We exclude much of this, anyway, if we define 'history' as the activities of humans ('natural history' has a quite different way of representing 'the past'). Indeed, until quite recently, history was only concerned with prominent individuals, whose exploits tended to provide more memorable portraits of the past than the repetitive everyday activity of the majority of folk. Further restrictions apply to our knowledge of and interest in the past when, as is nearly always the case, it is restricted to our own country or continent or culture. The advent of 'social history', which addresses the everyday activity of 'ordinary' people', especially neglected categories such as slaves, servants, women or children, and which comprises the vast bulk of human behaviour, has widened the scope of what we now think of as 'history', while globalization and the birth of multicultural societies makes us all think of the connectedness, and sometimes conflict, of the ways in which different people historicize events, even the same events.

Now we realize more than ever that any particular history will reflect certain interests, preconceptions and cultural values. This is because 'history' is the form in which we configure bits of human past to ourselves so as to comprehend it, engage with it and, not least, help us to define our identities through it. And the way we typically organize our images of the past is by means of narrative. Indeed, 'a history' is often used to mean 'a story'. 'Memory' has recently become a word used to label collective images of the past, and it is particularly useful because of the ways in which the mechanism of collective memory resembles individual memory: indeed, collective memories *are* in the end forms of individual memory, and because we can scientifically analyze how memory works, we can understand better how collective memories were formed and functioned in earlier societies. Indeed, it is particularly helpful to think of the contents of biblical stories as essentially collective memories. (On this topic, see more in Chapter 8.) Our parents tell us stories of life during their childhoods; our schoolteachers give us 'history lessons'; books, newspapers and magazines and the internet furnish us with a wealth of information about what has happened in the past; and television and radio programmes offer us dramatizations that mix real persons and events with invented ones. We also indulge in a form of history-making by sharing gossip, rumour, blogs and tweets, which we usually treat like knowledge while realizing that it is not necessarily true at all. This kind of information belongs to what we can call 'tradition'; it is 'handed on' among ourselves, until very often the original report is lost from view and we are left only with its wake. Folklore, legend, fable, urban myth and other kinds of 'knowledge' about the past are stories that we nearly always cannot verify and therefore do not really constitute *knowledge*. That is to say, what we are told may or may not have happened: we cannot say (and often do not care). In fact, nearly all of the contents of the Bible relate things we cannot verify. But historical knowledge allows room for – indeed, it is to a large extent determined by – the concept of probability. We might even define most of our histories as accounts of what *probably* happened – in our own assessment of probability.

Probability

What is it that we deem, on this formulation, as 'probable'? To begin with, we believe that persons and events in the past existed and happened. We can call this reality, or truth, if we like. We can even make statements of fact, such as that there was a kingdom known to some people as 'Israel' during the first half of the first millennium BCE, that people in the first century CE first starting claiming that Jesus of Nazareth was divine or was the Jewish Messiah (or both), and that Jerusalem was captured by Roman legions in 70 CE. But when we try to incorporate these statements into any kind of a *story*, we move away from fact and into 'history', that is, into the exercise of making sense. We select certain statements, or events, or persons, for our story of the past, and we choose to link them together in ways that make them mutually explicable. In short, we knit them into a story. Some historians might protest that they do not try and tell a story, but discuss themes and topics. However, what they are discussing inevitably implies that there is a story, even if the story is not explicitly told.

The creativity involved in historical reconstruction is nicely illustrated in cases involving conflicting stories about an event. Let us assume that however far they may agree they will also differ. What if we cannot determine which of the different accounts is closer to 'the truth' – bearing in mind that 'the truth' is actually something we don't know but are trying to find out. We can ask whether either account might be based on first-hand information, but even first-hand information may not be reliable, and we must always bear in mind that neither story is likely to have been constructed as a disinterested report. As is well known, modern conflicts generate opposing claims and reports from both sides, each of which, neutrals can see, serves the ideological interests of the participants. This was just as true in the ancient Near Eastern world of warring kingdoms and rulers anxious to enhance their reputation and prowess.

Forensic truth

Discussion of historical truth (especially in the case of the Bible) has often invoked the analogy of a court of law. In conducting a trial, there needs to be a notion of truth, though this is qualified by the principle that one side only needs to do the proving and that doubt will lead to a clear verdict: absence of proof of guilt means (in most cases) innocence.[2] But rather than accepting what witnesses say, the modern administration of justice in a civilized country encourages both sides to test witnesses and what they say, as well as using other kinds of evidence and, of course, arguments about what the evidence and the testimony means. From all this a verdict will ensue. The judge or jury will implicitly or explicitly conclude that something did (or did not) happen. But the verdict of a historian is a *judgement*. Justice is very much like history in the sense that the facts have to be collocated and what results is an informed deduction. Where the process is properly conducted, such judgements are accepted as the truth about the past, in the same way that a 'history' is accepted as imparting what really happened. But there is one important difference where the Bible is involved. Sometimes the implication of the trial analogy is that the Bible itself is in the dock, while the historian is the judge who must determine its innocence. Or even that the historian (if inclined not to believe everything the Bible relates) is a prosecuting or defending counsel. This leads to accusations of 'attacking' or 'defending' the Bible. But while the historical truth of the Bible may be relevant to a religious or theological debate, the historian does not regard the Bible as being in the dock. Failure to convey accurate historical recollection is not a crime. Moreover, it is not sensible to regard the contents of the Bible as either totally reliable or unreliable. What is important to remember is that the writers were usually not personal witnesses to what they wrote and in no position to provide us with what *we* demand by way of historical knowledge.

'Facts of history', then, is a slippery term: the same facts can generate different histories. Who the military victors in the war of

1914–18 were is fairly straightforward. But who 'won' the war? As
this is being written, on the centenary of the outbreak of that war, a
debate is raging about the causes of the war, whether it was a noble
war or a waste of lives, whether those in command were astute or
asinine, and most of all, who was responsible and to what degree
for starting a war that it seems no one really wanted. As a fact of
the past, we know much about this conflict. As a 'historical event',
however, we cannot entirely agree about it: its causes, consequences
and our 'memories' of it differ. Different (hi)stories can be told of
this conflict, and the different stories still evoke strong feelings. The
stories of the war are sometimes continuations of that war.

'Critical' history

In modern developed societies we are immersed both in informal,
'traditional' forms of 'knowledge' about the past and also in formal
knowledge. Formal knowledge of the past is what modern historians aim to acquire. It is what arises from the kind of procedures
just described as those of a court of law: it aims to establish past
events by the analysis of evidence that can be tested. An important
consequence of this procedure is that the 'knowledge' produced –
usually only to a degree of probability – can itself be challenged,
tested and revised using similar methods. In case this process
appears to be too mechanical and scientific, let us be clear that
'critical' or formal enquiry about the past is not a pure science, nor
merely a matter of applying rules. It can certainly be regarded as,
in part, a social science and modern historians increasingly operate
as social scientists – for example, in the use of social anthropology
and archaeology, or of any kind of statistical analysis. But if some
'historical facts' can be discovered in this way,[3] the process by
which these are endowed with their significance by creating a story
entails much more uncertainty. Causality, which is perhaps the
main device by which events are so linked, is not, as in the pure
sciences, capable of being experimentally demonstrated. Instead
historians have to appeal to what they regard as analogous cases
or an agreed understanding of how humans normally behave.
But there are no fixed laws to govern these calculations, and here
especially the historian is appealing to an assessment of probability.

In fact, this may be a good place to point out that probability is exactly what proves that a critical history cannot correspond exactly to the 'real past'. The critical historian must argue for whatever seems the most probable. And yet we cannot fail to be aware that improbable things will occasionally happen. Critical histories will always be histories of the probable, even when assessments of the probable will differ amongst historians. Beyond known 'facts', historical knowledge, and explanations of historical events, is knowledge of probabilities. This is our 'historical knowledge', and clearly it must be wrong in cases where an improbability occurred. But on what grounds can a critical historian argue that an improbability occurred in any one instance? How could any disagreement on this point be resolved? Most gripping stories have to employ the devices of coincidence and unexpected fortune or setback. It is a generic feature of most storytelling. By contrast, the historian has to fall back on the mundane, though irony is entirely permissible!

The ancient historian is, much more than the historian of modern times, bereft of a good deal of first-hand information such as photographs, record files, magazines, newspapers or recordings. However, what we call the 'historical period' of human existence begins when written records appear that point us to past events and as these become more numerous, they play a larger role compared with inference from inanimate objects, which furnish, our only traces of prehistoric human life (though the products of human art and technology can be revealing). The 'biblical historian', whose interest lies in a particular twelve centuries of Palestine's past, can draw on a quite respectable amount of written sources – of which the biblical texts comprise the largest part. In addition, there are several other texts, including inscriptions, that impinge on this bit of history. What needs to be clarified, however – and this is not always explicitly done by historians – is what quality of knowledge these texts represent. Were the authors themselves witnesses, or are they repeating what they heard from others? Are their accounts produced by careful reflection or by any kind of arguments or reasoning? Is their intention to give the reader an objective description of what transpired? In other words, does any kind of 'critical history' appear in the writings that provide the historian with sources?

Most indications suggest that the biblical texts do *not*, on these criteria, convey a high quality of historical knowledge about the events they describe. But this is true of most ancient writing about the past, not least because no one had much interest in fulfilling such criteria. How much better are modern critical histories, and in what ways? To begin with, they form a distinct genre of narrative, with its own rhetoric and conventions. The critical historian may try to tell, or imply, a story as simply as possible, but we also expect some indication of the source of the information and we assume the historian will have assessed its credibility. We will not expect to read the thoughts or speeches of the characters, unless these have been accurately transcribed; instead the historian may deduce the thoughts of protagonists from their actions. Again, the purpose of a critical history is primarily to instruct and not to entertain, though we must not distinguish too rigorously between these, because entertainment can be a form of instruction and vice versa. It may also be the case that the historian wishes to convey a moral about human behaviour through the writing of a history. Perfectly acceptable, so long as we judge the moral to be drawn and not imposed.

What characterizes critical history most clearly, perhaps, to modern readers becomes clear in its distinction from a similar genre, the historical novel. This genre employs scenes, events and sometimes even characters that cannot be verified as ever having existed in the past, while the artistry of plot construction and elaboration of character profiles, converting historical figures into characters, creates a more vivid, but also more imagined, scenario. But many historical novelists undertake careful research to ensure that they do not make factual errors: that is, they aim to avoid describing things as happening that could not have happened or that we know did not happen. If a historical novel relates what *could* have happened, even when we realize that real life does not exhibit drama or plot in the way described, then it stands quite close to critical history. Each genre is, after all, a constructed narrative.

But for premodern times, at any rate, we have to forget any distinction between a critical reproduction of the past and a novelistic one. Writing about the past in earlier periods of human civilization aimed at purposes other than factual instruction, such as entertainment, moral instruction, propaganda, identity-building and self-aggrandizement. Critical evaluation of sources was not often possible, either. This makes our use of the words 'history-writing' and 'historiography' problematic. Do we insist on reserving these words for what we understand as critical histories, or can we apply them to any attempt to write a story about the past, or at least a story that the reader might be able to accept as what could have occurred? There is no agreement on this. But in any case, what is important to grasp in looking at 'histories' written in the past is the implicit understanding between writer and reader regarding the meaning of what is being said about the past – and indeed, what 'the past' means to both of them.

The modern critical historian also differs from the ancient, however, in the understanding of human activity itself. What do we now believe to be the engine of history? Has it a plot or purpose? Why do things happen the way they do, and not some other way?[4] Like most people, historians now understand the human story as being generated by human behaviour and human nature. Alongside the natural environment to which we must respond but which we also shape, it is humanity itself that drives events. But until the modern era, the fate of humans, individually and collectively, was believed to be determined by supernatural beings, whose nature and intentions could only be partly perceived, and this by means of divination. To call this cultural assumption 'religion' invokes a slippery word, but certainly such beliefs hampered the development of what we now call a 'sense of history', an awareness of the past as objectively different but as causally and temporally linked to the here and now. 'History' was not an evolving process of human interaction but either the outworking of a divine plan or the outcome of fairly wilful activity by deities. Divine direction and even intervention in human affairs was accepted as normal, and recourse was regularly sought to divination before engaging in ventures whose outcome was uncertain – warfare, trade and illness. No kind of critical history can be offered in terms of divine plans and interventions, because such causation can never be proven.

So histories of modern times invoke neither supernatural explanations nor supernatural occurrences. Unless we wish to imagine the ancient past as being of a different order, happening in a different world, from our own, we exclude such things from our own ancient histories. Except, we should add, for histories of 'ancient Israel', where even in the twentieth century, apparently serious historians would invoke the mind of the biblical god to explain the course of events. In doing so, these writers were, perhaps even deliberately, creating a separate world, one in which a 'sacred history' was being played out. Meanwhile historians of other part of the world, ancient and modern, were explaining the past purely in terms of human motivation. 'Biblical history' has, however, come in the last few decades to join the rest of human history, which seeks to understand humanity and not the ways of gods. In one sense, nevertheless, the historian of 'ancient Israel' is pursuing a very special course. The Bible constitutes a resource that the historian of this period simply cannot ignore, and for the analysis of which special tools are required. The biblical historian has to be, among other things, a very good textual exegete. But 'biblical historians' (the term should not properly be used) should employ principles and methods that are no different from historians of other periods, for the history of this time and place is part of a wider human history into which it must ultimately be integrated. Even that truth was grasped by the writers of Genesis 1–11!

3

Origins of Ancient Historiography

We now take a look at ancient writing about the past, and ask how, in the absence of the kinds of documentation that enable modern historians to write critical histories, the first historians attempted to go beyond 'traditional' (hearsay) knowledge about the past and formulate the question: 'what *really* happened'?

'Historiography' is not the only genre that narrates the human past. There has been endless debate over how it is to be defined, and whether there is historiography in the Bible. Does it entail awareness of the concept of 'what really happened', that is, a past that can be known, accessed through direct evidence, or reconstructed by means of critically comparing and interrogating stories to arrive at the 'true' account? Where past *is* known only in the form of stories told by persons who themselves, the very idea of something that existed objectively, apart from the stories, does not necessarily arise. Historiography arises from a shift in the reception of a story, from an aesthetic judgement, assessing the skill of the storyteller, or an ideological judgement, assessing the accordance of the story with one's prejudices, to a notion of truth: did things happen as the story narrates it? This question betrays a 'historical consciousness', an awareness of a past independent of the stories that narrate it and an interest in that past rather than in the story itself. It may be useful to reserve the term 'historiography' to any large-scale narrative about this 'real' past, whether or not the narrative itself conveys any actual knowledge about it.

What we cannot do is to make historicity a criterion of historiography, because ultimately no ancient historiographer has adequate knowledge and can guarantee to be right about the past.

If 'historiography' is minimally defined it a certain genre of writing, a large-scale narrative about the human past, we can speak of 'biblical historiography', as we shall. But if we want a more restrictive definition according to which historiography narrates, or attempts to narrate 'what really happened' then we may also expect a narrative that arises from investigation, enquiry. Indeed, our use of the word 'history' derives from the Greek word for 'enquiry': *historiē*. This is how Herodotus and others named their work (in exactly the same way our words 'gospel' and 'apocalyptic' derive from words from the opening of Mark's story of Jesus (Greek *euangelion*, 'good news' and the last book of the New Testament (Greek *apokalypsis*, 'revelation'). Applying this criterion probably leaves biblical narrative out of account, because, even if its authors were trying to write what had really occurred, as Halpern (1996) argued, and used written sources such as royal annals, can we say that they used any criteria to assess the truth of what they were saying? Did they perceive a gap between received sources and a past reality to which these sources claimed to refer? The general consensus on these narratives is rather that their criterion was how history should have been, or who it should be perceived, in order to support the authors' view of the present and the future. This is not to say that they did not occasionally describe what actually happened; but historicity of itself does not make a work historiography, unless that history is the outcome of enquiry. Connected with the notion of 'enquiry' is the identification of the author as someone who vouches for the truth of what is being written. Marincola (1997) has described and compared the kinds of 'rhetoric of authority' that various classical historians used. As Noll (2001: 71–780) has explained, this rhetoric is absent from the biblical historiographies. The later attributions of authorship to Moses, Samuel and Ezra is perhaps a response to this 'rhetoric of authority'. If we don't know how it is that the writer knows, we can still recognize what we read as 'historiography' but can we accept what is said as 'history'?

The double heritage of historiography

The emergence of historiography in the ancient world can be described in more than one way, and in each case it develops from other genres, both formal and informal. It can be understood as a product of monarchy, and here we focus attention on the ancient Near East. The other way of looking at it is in terms of an attempt to explain the nature of the world; here we look to the Greek colonies of the western part of Asia Minor. In his *In Search of History* (1983), John Van Seters provides an excellent review of both perspectives in exploring the origins of history writing in Greece, Egypt and Mesopotamia, the civilizations that surrounded Palestine and dominated most of its history. He adopts the definition of history given by Jan Huizinga: 'the intellectual form in which a civilization renders account to itself of its past' (Huizinga 1936: 9) and explains that the 'nation' was, in the ancient world, usually personified by the monarch. In an ancient monarchic society, the deeds of the monarch become identified with those of the nation (the biblical books of Kings are a good example of this), and at moment the royal power acquires certain level, which includes the use of scribes in his service, 'history' as Van Seters has defined it, can emerge alongside the various kinds of stories of the past that circulated as what we might call 'folklore'. Van Seters also notes that such folkloristic narrations of the past, through being not merely repeated, but also varied in the retelling, tend to 'overwrite' themselves, obliterating distinctions between past and present, while literary texts, being tangible objects, furnish a fixed, concrete relic of the past from which its difference from the present can at least be in principle observed. On this explanation, historiography belongs with other forms of royal glorification such as dedication and victory inscriptions, annals and law codes.

Ancient Near East: Royal genres

King lists

Among the earliest genres of Mesopotamian writing about the past is the Sumerian King List (extant in several version), a text that also illustrates very well how the presentation of the past served the ruler. Originating in the third millennium BCE, it records kings of Sumer (in the south of Mesopotamia) and the lengths of their reigns, which, like the biblical humans before the Flood, were abnormally long. The list asserts that kingship was handed down by the gods, and would pass from one city to another as political hegemony shifted. There is a striking similarity here with the way in which the book of Daniel claims that the high god bestows sovereignty on one king and one empire after another. A direct link between Daniel and the king lists is unlikely, but what binds them together is the ideological thread that accepts kingship as the divinely legitimized form of rule, created and sanctioned by the gods. This notion was not only universal in the ancient Near East, but persisted in parts of Europe until the seventeenth or eighteenth century. It pervades the Hebrew Bible, but with an interesting angle: the loss of native monarchy was compensated for in several ways: by transferring royal sovereignty to the imperial king (as Isaiah 45 does to Cyrus), to the one god (as do several Psalms), and by expressing a hope in a future king, a belief not very prominent in the Bible itself but revived in the proliferation of 'messianic' figures in the Greco-Roman era.

The Sumerian King List – like the genealogies of humanity in the opening chapters of Genesis – provides a schematic way of representing the timespan between past and present. The measurement is of course wildly inaccurate, but so much the better, so as to extend the beginnings of human society into a very remote past. The monarchs of the King List are in some cases identifiable with historical figures, unlike the names in Genesis, but in both the Sumerian and biblical schemes the distant past is separated from the world of the present by a great flood, a fact that demonstrates – as has long been recognized – the dependence of the Genesis story of human origins on the Mesopotamian story. The great Flood creates a kind of boundary between the world of human experience and a mythical world characterized by direct interaction between by gods and humans and including half-human and half-divine heroes (of which we see a trace in Genesis 6.1–4).

Royal inscriptions

Royal inscriptions, unlike the king lists, derive from the monarchs themselves, and include several genres. Campaign annals list the military achievements of the king on his seasonal expeditions, among which the Assyrian corpus is paramount. These texts were displayed in the royal palaces, not to be read, but to impress the visitor, presumably aware of what they were. Victory and commemorative monuments are occasional inscriptions erected at the place where the events occurred, for example at the scene of a battle, or on the site of a temple. Law codes (again we can see the influence of these in the books of Exodus and Deuteronomy) represent the king's claim to transmit divinely sanctioned laws for the people. What such writings have in common is the goal of establishing or glorifying the reputation of the king as builder, lawgiver or warrior – these being the major duties of a king in fulfilment of his divine commission as creator of order on earth.

Omen lists

Omen lists represent the most widely attested ancient Mesopotamian genre, again produced under royal patronage, which correlated observed omens such as a comet or eclipse or an abnormal birth with subsequent events such as a plague, assassination or military defeat, of which these signs were believed to be premonitions. Each record usually consisted of a protasis and apodosis (if ... then ...). The lists deserve our attention because they intimate the beginnings of a kind of order or law in historical events; in fact it seems (see below) that they are the precursors, both formally and intellectually, of the Babylonian chronicle. For even if these omens were seen as manifestations of divine intentions, the lists imply belief in a regular correlation, not of an entailed cause and effect, but of a direct link between something understood as a sign and what it signified. Producing the lists enabled the special guilds of diviners to augment a simple enquiry of the deity by means of a database, a body of empirical knowledge that demonstrated a pattern in the occurrence of events. Such observations led to the Babylonians' unrivalled understanding of astronomy, in which the regular behaviour of the celestial bodies was recognized and carefully recorded. Divination institutionalized the view that what happens in human existence depends on divine will and activity, but the omen lists show that this was not understood to be purely arbitrary, or at least not unpredictable. We should certainly take note of this view, which explains why we do not find our modern kind of history in ancient texts. If all events (or even some) are the outcome of divine motivation, history amounts to little more than celestial politics. It may nevertheless strike us as unlikely that kings or their subjects were really unaware of a natural causation in human affairs, even if the rules were divinely scripted (read the book of Proverbs!) Divinations performed for kings before their military campaigns no doubt reflected in part the intentions of the king himself and the prudence of the diviners. Moreover, a degree of human initiative is possible in shaping events, because, for example, the gods can be provoked to good or ill by the freely taken actions of humans. This recognition brings us much closer to our modern understanding of historical cause and effect, and in the books of Kings, for instance, a scheme whereby national (as exemplified by royal) obedience to the divine will is the determinant of the nation's fate enshrines the principle that human action can indeed determine the future.

Chronicles

The chronicle is a genre undertaken by royal officials that records sequentially the names and deeds of kings, and as such obviously constitutes a step towards a continuous, chronologically ordered narrative of the past. Starting in the second millennium, the Assyrian kings appointed annually an official called a *limmu*, after whom each year could be named: this procedure offered an alternative to the system of dating years by the king's reign (as in the biblical narratives and generally elsewhere). The extant *limmu* lists in fact allow modern historians to establish absolute dates for Assyrian history from 911 to 631 BCE, and for each year a brief record of events is provided. The Babylonian Chronicle (or Chronicles) is represented on a tablet recording events from 605 to 594 BCE, that is, during the reign of Nebuchadrezzar II, including the capture of Jerusalem, which we can date in our modern calendar to 16 March 598.

The form of the Babylonian Chronicle has an interesting resemblance to the contents of omen lists, from which its form may derive. The format of the Chronicle resembles the apodoses of omens (that is, it omits the 'if') and, although they are concerned with the recent past, they seem in turn to have prompted an interest in chronicles of the distant past (Van Seters 1983: 91). The authors of this Chronicle undoubtedly belonged to the world of diviners, but it is widely agreed that its character is academic and did not serve the usual royal propaganda functions. Perhaps, as Van Seters claims, the purpose of this Chronicle reflects an objective interest in antiquity; but alternatively, what the authors are seeking is a pattern, a meaning, in the course of events, in accordance with the purposes of the omen list. In either case, it can be argued that divinatory activity leads quite naturally towards the borders of historiography, the Chronicle itself providing the kind of accurate data that would permit a narrative of 'what really happened' to be composed, however limited its scope.

Apocalyptic

The omen list, and the culture of divination that it serves, is also the basis of another formal genre of writing about the past known as 'apocalyptic'. 'Apocalyptic' is now used of the end of the world, but the ancient genre concerned all manner of secrets about the past as well as the future, and indeed about the celestial world too. The book of Daniel offers a few excellent examples of this genre, which demonstrates a mantic (that is, divinatory) view of the process of history, in which the high god disposes earthly sovereignty to one human king after another, offers a sign in the form of dreams or writing on a wall, and reveals the meaning of the omen to the Jewish sage. The underlying view in this book is that history is predetermined by the unalterable purpose of a single god, but rather than by the regular mechanical means of divination (star-gazing, inspecting entrails of animals, dreaming), the future is here revealed by vision or oracle to a chosen mediator. Reviews of the past in this genre of writing typically serve to expose the scheme of history that explains the (troublesome) present but also, when the revelation is ascribed to a seer who lived before these events, to establish his credentials as a reliable predictor of the future. The apocalypses in Daniel express the concept of a world-history, a single plot embracing all events and leading to a predetermined end. According to this genre, history has a determinate meaning, and one that humans cannot influence since the meaning was devised long ago. Apocalypses certainly have a mythical character and may use mythical imagery (see Daniel 7 and 8). But the myth here is the myth of history itself, an understanding of what drives national or world events. Here, where human behaviour plays little or no role in influencing the future, we can see worked out a purely divinatory philosophy of history.

As we shall presently see, biblical historiographies share some features of this divinatory kind of understanding of the past as preordained, but they do not exclude human behaviour as a factor, and so comprise a rather different understanding of meaningful human historical action, one that brings us close to modern canons of history writing.

Greek historiography: 'Enquiry'

A second (and more widely recognized) root of the origin of historiography lies in an enterprise of scientific enquiry into the nature of all things: the composition of the physical world, its geography, and its past. Before the arrival of the first of such historians among the Ionian Greeks, Homer and Hesiod had written great epic poems, in which, as Herodotus put it, they 'created a theogony for the Greeks, gave the gods titles, assigned their various honours and arts, and established their forms'. These writers are given the name of 'logographers', and they produced various kinds of prose writing (something of an innovation): myths, accounts of travels in foreign lands, local stories, especially founding legends, family histories and genealogies and lists of kings. Importantly, they combined these different sorts of information to produce what can be seen as an immediate precursor of the more systematic and wide-ranging *Histories* of Herodotus. The writings of these logographers are no longer preserved, but they are quoted and plagiarized by later historians.

Hecataeus of Miletus (550–476) is a transitional figure between the logographer and the historian. We know of two of his works:

one (*Geneologica*) being an account of Greek mythology, the other (*Periegesis*) describing the peoples to be met in voyaging around Europe and Asia. Attempts, then, to organize knowledge of the world's past and its present extent. Perhaps it is he who deserves the title of 'father of history', but the honour has been bestowed rather on Herodotus of Halicarnassus. Before describing his work, we should note that interest in the origins of the gods and in the population of the known world (the lands surrounding the Mediterranean) is part of a wider curiosity on the part of others from Ionia and its neighbouring region in Asia Minor, who are often regarded as the founders of philosophy in their goal of explaining the natural world in terms of physical laws and not mythological tales. In Hecataeus and even more so in Herodotus (c. 484–425 BCE) we can see this curiosity as the driving force behind both writing about the past as a meaningful story and also in seeing the story as extending into the lives of non-Greeks and realizing – as Herodotus never tires of reminding his readers and listeners – that the Greeks are not necessarily with the oldest or greatest of civilizations.

Both Hecataeus and Herodotus employ the word *historiē*, 'enquiry, research' to describe their accounts, and both also travelled widely in their 'researches'. Both spend most of their time relating stories they heard from local sources, but they do not rehearse these credulously, and they seek to consult those they think best qualified to know the truth. Hecataeus declared, tellingly, that 'I write what I deem true; for the stories of the Greeks are manifold and seem to me ridiculous', while Herodotus often comments on the credibility of what he is told, and far from being chauvinistic, considered the Egyptians an older race than the Greeks. One factor in this awareness of, and interest in, non-Greek lands and their stories may be that while the Ionians and their neighbours were 'Hellenes' (Greeks), they had lived under Persian rule from the middle of the sixth century. Early in the fifth century these colonies had revolted, initiating the prolonged war between Persians and Greeks that is the central subject of Herodotus' *Histories*. For him, no account of the past could be confined to the story of one people.

Herodotus's 'enquiry' took him all over the known world (known to him, anyway), embracing the origins of many human civilizations. As already noted, he asked the people whom he thought knew best, and often sought out more than one opinion. On the different stories he relates of the same event, he sometimes lets the reader decide and sometimes expresses his own preference, usually giving a reason. He declares at the outset his purpose in writing such a 'history':

> This is the outcome of the inquiry of Herodotus of Halicarnassos, so that that neither the deeds of humans may be forgotten by lapse of time, nor the great and wonderful works performed by Greeks and non-Greeks, may lose their renown; and especially that the causes for which these waged war with one another may be remembered.

It was important to him, then, that the great deeds of the past be remembered, not from disinterested curiosity, but because an accurate memory was important. Herodotus is not yet a modern critical historian: he accepts that injustice and hubris can provoke divine intervention, and makes reference to the use of oracles in a way that implies belief in their efficacy. But the contrast between this kind of 'enquiring' historiography and the examples given earlier from the ancient Near East, including the Hebrew Bible, is fairly straightforward. There, we are not told where the information comes from, or who the author is; we encounter no critical judgement on any story, and very little attempt at understanding human motivation except in very crude terms. There is scant interest in the affairs of any other nation other than as pawns or foils in what is essentially an account of dealings between the king and its god. In recent years (see below) some scholars have nevertheless suggested that the biblical historiographies are dependent upon Herodotus. This is not chronologically impossible, and there is no real historiographic genre found in other ancient Near Eastern texts (those discussed above fall short) evident in the ancient Near East before the Hellenistic era (late fourth century); indeed, for Persian history itself we are still hugely dependent on Greek writers. The dating of the biblical historiographies is from this point of view crucial. The claim that the Bible contains the earliest historiography remains to be substantiated, though, as already stated, such a statement depends a lot on what 'historiography' is chosen to mean.

Greek influence on biblical historiography?

While some parts of the Bible have long been assigned to a possible Hellenistic date (Daniel, Ecclesiastes, Chronicles, Malachi, certain Psalms), the view that the contents of the Bible as a whole emanate from the fourth century or later was prompted by N. P. Lemche (1993), who stated specifically that 'the writers who invented the "history of Israel" seem to have modeled their history on a Greek pattern' (p. 183). More specific arguments that Herodotus' *Histories* provided such a model were produced by Nielsen (1997) and Wesselius (2002), while Gmirkin (2006) argued for parallels between the Babylonian mythological materials preserved in Berossus (c. 278 BCE) and the Genesis stories, and Egyptian records preserved by Manetho (c. 285–280 BCE) and the story in Exodus. To explain these, Gmirkin infers that the third century BCE translation of the Pentateuch into Greek made in Alexandria actually represents the original composition of the whole text. The biblical narratives therefore reflect the events of the third century BCE, especially the conquests of Alexander and his successors. Wajdebaum's slightly different stance on this issue (2011) argues that Genesis–Kings is the work of a single author seeking to counter the powerful Greek cultural tradition, represented especially by Herodotus and Plato. Thompson and Wajdebaum have more recently produced an edited volume containing contributions from some other scholars who suggest some Greek parallels but do not necessarily support the idea of large-scale borrowing of biblical material from Greek. A useful discussion of the issue from many angles (but before some of the above contributions were published) is available in Grabbe 2001.

The suggestion of such influence on the scale proposed by these authors is generally rejected (Barstad 2002) responded to Lemche's proposal), but, as already observed, the chronology is not such a problem as it appears to some. Herodotus lived in the fifth century, which is certainly not too late for the production of the biblical historiographies, and one curious but perhaps telling detail is the use of the Hebrew word *midrash* twice in Chronicles to denote some kind of written account (2 Chron. 13.22; 24.27). These are the only biblical occurrences of a word that in the rabbinic writings means 'commentary'. Its root meaning, however, is 'enquire', which could make it an exact translation of the Greek *historiē* which (see above) Herodotus names his own work. Like a number of issues in modern scholarly discussion over biblical historiography, the whole issue has been unnecessarily framed in black-and-white terms. There are several plausible sections of biblical writing that invoke a Greek parallel, however this is to be explained. Two obvious examples are the story of Jephthah and his daughter in Judges 11 (compare the fate(s) of Iphigenia, the daughter of Agamemnon) and the last days of Saul, when he is visited by a shade from the underworld that predicts his death, and falls in battle by his own hand. In the latter case there is no single direct comparison, but such portents and suicide are typical of Greek hero stories and unusual if not unique within biblical narrative. Here we have a tragedy on classical lines. 'Greek influence' does not necessarily indicate a Hellenistic date, either. Greek traders and mercenaries (along with 'Sea Peoples' who settled in the Palestinian coastal plain) made their presence felt in the Levant from at least the beginning of the Iron Age.

Yet if the biblical historiographies are in any way inspired by their Greek counterparts, the crucial features of enquiry and authentication are lacking. The cultural and intellectual matrix of the biblical historiographies seems to owe something to both Greek and Near Eastern cultures, which is not surprising if we recognize that from the fifth century onwards the two worlds engage even more closely than previously, and not just in the Persian desire to conquer Greece (as they did Asia Minor, at the time Herodotus was writing!). The culture that we call 'Hellenism' can more accurately be described as a fusion of Greek and Near Eastern than as an imposition of Greek upon Near Eastern. 'Persian-Hellenistic', or even 'Persian-Greek', is a better term for the fifth and fourth centuries BCE. It is unfortunate that our sources about this period (Hebrew, Persian, Greek) are so meagre. But a great deal of the biblical historiography, in its final form if not its original creation, actually emanates from these centuries.

4

Biblical Historiography

In the biblical story of the past from the Creation of the world in Genesis 1, through the Flood, the call of Abraham, the destruction of Sodom, the crossing of the sea and up to the fall of Jericho, the killing of Goliath, and on to the kings of Israel and Judah, we find a continuous narrative. Should we regard all of this as biblical historiography? But evidently the first eleven chapters are stories emanating from a mythical past. Even the stories of the rest of Genesis are episodic, and have been regarded by many biblical scholars as folklore. What about the Exodus, at an unspecified time under an unspecified pharaoh and including divine miracles and encounters? Many different genres of writing about the past are combined, and perhaps also different perceptions of what the past is or was.

The 'first' and 'second' histories

There are two large-scale narratives about 'Israel' in the Hebrew Bible. The first, from Genesis to 2 Kings, presents a continuous story from Creation to the end of the kingdom of Judah. But biblical scholars do not regard this narrative as the work of a single writer or editor, or even as a single work. The contents are in fact separated in the biblical canon, with the story from Creation to the death of Moses comprising the Pentateuch or Torah, the 'Books of Moses' (Genesis–Deuteronomy) while Joshua–Kings, from the end of Moses' career to the deportation to Babylonia, comprises the 'Former Prophets' of the Hebrew canon ('Historical Books' in the Greek and Latin Bible). However, the original boundaries of these composite works are not necessarily as the canon fixed them. If we distinguish the two components in terms of theme and subject matter, it is perhaps more appropriate to end the first story with Joshua. On this division, the first is a history of the birth and infancy of a twelve-tribe 'nation' or 'people' up to its corporate possession of a land, while the second deals with two pieces of territory, Judah and Israel, and two kingdoms with corresponding names. On this basis, Judges belongs with the latter, because it displays some links to 1 Samuel (the figure of the judge; the Judah–Benjamin rivalry) but, more importantly, it begins with an alternative account of conquest than the unified assault in Joshua, an account that favours Judah at the expense of the other tribes. Once separated in this way, it can be seen that these two stories portray different 'Israels', the first a twelve-tribe nation, the second two 'houses' and then two kingdoms/ Within Judges and 1 Samuel there is a sort of transition by means of an emphasis on twelve individual tribes that also separates out Judah from the others, though this separation is never described nor explained.

The second narrative comprises the books of Chronicles, Ezra and Nehemiah, which appear in this sequence in Christian Bibles but not in the Hebrew Bible, where Chronicles comes at the end of the canon (and thus out of chronological sequence). All these books were until the last fifty years or so thought to be the work of a single author, partly because the final verses of Chronicles are repeated at the opening of Ezra. But it is now widely accepted (on the basis of work by Japhet (1989) and Williamson (1977)) that when seen from the perspective of the 'Israel' they describe, they are from different kinds of authors. A further complication is that while Ezra and Nehemiah are two separate books in the Christian Bible, in the Hebrew Bible they are treated as a single unit (see more on this problem in Chapter 7). Chronicles seems to be an attempt to extend the single unified twelve-tribe people of the Pentateuch into the monarchic era as well. The events narrated in Genesis–1 Samuel, up to the death of Saul, are recast in a summary form, almost entirely through genealogies, and the action begins only in Chapter 10 with Saul's final battle and the arrival of David. By this means the bitter rivalry, occupying most of 1 Samuel, between Saul and David and between the 'houses' of Judah and Israel, and the bloody struggle to secure David as king over both is not found. Saul's family is not wiped out and his tribe, Benjamin, receives more recognition thereafter. Nor is there any account of the section in 2 Samuel containing David's domestic troubles with Amnon, Bathsheba and Absalom. The 'Israel' of Ezra and Nehemiah, by contrast, consists only of Judahites, and not necessarily all of those, either, and portrays the leaders of Samaria as hostile outsiders.

Chronicles minimizes the division of 'Israel' into two kingdoms, so that the kingdom over which David and Solomon reign is not a 'united monarchy' of two 'houses' but one indivisible kingdom. Nothing of the history of the seceded kingdom called Israel is narrated except for its beginning and end; it is presented as a temporary state of affairs, a punishment for Solomon's behaviour, and when this kingdom comes to an end with the fall of its capital Samaria, the unity of 'Israel' is fully restored under its rightful Davidic king and his capital and temple in Jerusalem. Chronicles also understands its 'Israel' as a nation defined by religion and cult, not political identity. The 'house' promised to David through the prophet Nathan is now not the dynasty but the temple, whose design and liturgy Chronicles attributes to David. The word *qahal* (translated 'congregation') is often used as well as *'am* ('people') of this 'Israel', and (as in 2 Chron. 20) the king is a religious leader more than a military or even political one.

The books of Ezra and Nehemiah seem to be intended (whether by the author of Ezra or by a later editor) to follow on from Chronicles by beginning with the last words of 2 Chronicles. They are the only historiographical books in the Hebrew scriptures dealing with the post-monarchic era and they relate the reconstitution of Judah as an 'Israel' after the conquest of Babylon by Cyrus and the imperial permission for Judahites to return. As a result of their efforts the rebuilding of Jerusalem's temple is finally completed, along with its walls, and the city once again becomes the capital of the province.

From this review of the biblical 'Histories' we can conclude that while the different compositions disagree in a few (and perhaps not very important) respects about the events of the past, they do, on analysis, exhibit quite important variations in their understanding of what constitutes Israel'. This will be examined more closely in Chapter 6, and here we just observe that the origins and purpose of biblical historiography may well have to do with a concern to define how Judah and Israel are related or should be related. The modern historian cannot speak any longer simply of 'biblical Israel', far less assume an 'ancient Israel' on the basis of the biblical texts. Rather, the production of these different portraits of 'Israel' becomes itself a historical issue: what historical circumstances explain the apparent combat over 'Israelite' identity?

Historiographies of the monarchy

In speaking of 'biblical historiography' current scholarly discussion therefore generally confines itself to two compositions, known as the 'Deuteronomistic History' and the 'Chronicler's History'. We shall concentrate first on these. According to the model proposed by Martin Noth and still widely accepted (Noth 1943 [ET 1981], 1948 [ET 1972]), Deuteronomy provided an introduction to a narrative of Israel in its land, from conquest to expulsion (Joshua–Kings). This history played out the principles set out in Deuteronomy – that possession of the land depended on observance of the covenant, especially faithfulness to the cult of its god, and abstinence from foreign influences. In its present form, however, Deuteronomy has been incorporated as the concluding part of the Pentateuch, the end of Moses' life having been shifted from the closing of Numbers, and it has been furnished with another introduction looking backwards to the contents of the preceding books. Hence as it stands, Deuteronomy constitutes a link between the life and work of Moses and the events that follow, suggesting the intention on the part of an editor to weld Genesis to Kings in the History just described.

The composition of the books of Joshua–Kings remains, however, a matter of considerable and growing disagreement. The 'Deuteronomistic History', according to Noth, was the unified work of a single editor or group of editors, with a clear theme and programme. He suggested that it was written in Judah after the deportations of 596 and 586. This thesis has subsequently been modified by the recognition of more than one edition. One theory has a first redaction taking place in the reign of Josiah late in the seventh century, and a second edition in the sixth century, among the deportees in Babylonia. A second places the initial composition as Noth, in the sixth century, but proposes further later redactions (for an excellent account, see Römer 2007). But recently the view of a unified composition has begun to be challenged. This issue, along with the date of Deuteronomy itself, is one of the crucial literary problems facing the modern historian.

On the unity and dating of the second historiography there is less disagreement. Chronicles and Kings cover more or less the same ground, and with a great deal of common text, and it has been generally accepted that Chronicles bases its account on Samuel–Kings. Graeme Auld, however (1994), has suggested that both are based on an original account to which Chronicles might actually be closer. The matter is complicated by the fact that the Hebrew text of Samuel–Kings has almost certainly itself undergone editing that Chronicles has not, leaving Chronicles in many cases with the earlier version of their parallel text. Neither the story of David's reign told in 2 Samuel 9–20 and 1 Kings 1–2 nor the Elijah and Elisha stories are in Chronicles, but were they left out for one reason, or added to Samuel–Kings for another reason?

From a formal point of view, both Joshua–Kings and Chronicles can be seen as sequels to the Pentateuchal story: 1 Chron. 1–9 is a kind of recapitulation, or perhaps a genealogical reduction, of the story, while if Deuteronomy were originally part of a longer 'Deuteronomistic History', that historiography begins with a rehearsal of the other four books of Moses. As to whether Chronicles is also a rewriting of Samuel–Kings, in which case it is not a great deal more than another edition, or a separate revision of a shared source, we can now see more clearly than we used to that between them lie quite fundamental ideological differences. They are not only different histories but histories of different Israels.

The Pentateuch

Although the books of Moses are not primarily approached as historiography but rather as 'Law', Genesis–Deuteronomy offers a continuous narrative. The construction of this narrative is the subject of much scholarly disagreement, but we can agree that most of the stories in Genesis are constructed from episodic components of myth and then family history, set in a time that cannot be correlated with any other historical epoch and indeed only quite loosely juxtaposed. The Joseph story, by contrast, reads like a polished novella. Deuteronomy is recognized as an originally autonomous composition, and the same may be true for Leviticus. Exodus and Numbers seem to be made up of several different kinds of material. So how did they come together to form a single story? And was this early in its development or a late piece of editing? Do we see sources running through more than one book, or independent themes (or even books) being finally stuck together? Pentateuchal criticism has always been a contentious matter, hardly made easier by the recognition in recent decades that it is mostly not based on events nor, probably, even early traditions.

This story tells of a people that, unlike others, inherited its customs and worship not from natural evolution but by direct divine command. Unlike the two historiographies just mentioned, and unlike Ezra–Nehemiah (see below), this story does not express viewpoints promoted within the province of Judah/Yehud, nor does it even mention the city of Jerusalem. It belongs, in more or less identical form, to the scriptural canon of both Jews and Samaritans, and its existence attests a once fraternal relationship between the two provinces that contradicts the negative attitude towards Samaria implied in most of the remainder of the Jewish biblical canon. The Jewish and Samaritan versions of the story are not, however, without evidence of rivalry. The most important variation occurs in Deut. 27.4–5, which in the Jewish text reads:

> So when you have crossed over the Jordan, you shall set up these stones, about which I am commanding you today, on Mount Ebal, and you shall cover them with plaster. And you shall build an altar there to Yhwh your God, an altar of stones on which you have not used an iron tool.

The Samaritan text reads 'Mount Gerizim', and there is little doubt now that it is the Jewish version that has been amended, in order to remove scriptural justification for the Samarian temple built on that site.[1] Deuteronomy's stipulation that the worship of Yhwh would take place at a designated 'place I shall choose' appears to have been understood in both Judah and Samaria as stipulating one temple only, and recent excavations on Gerizim have uncovered the Samarian temple, apparently built in the fifth century – that is, about the same time as the new temple in Jerusalem.

There can be no doubt that within the province of Samaria the identity of 'Israel' was preserved, as it still is among the Samaritans. There are traces outside the Pentateuch of a persistent Israelite identity there, too. In the book of Ezekiel, the twelve tribes are reconfigured in a way quite different from the Pentateuchal arrangement, and with a new sanctuary at their centre. The book also displays a uniquely even-handed attitude towards Samaria and Jerusalem, regarding both as equally sinful. Additionally, in the early chapters of the book of Jeremiah are oracles to the 'house of Israel' which, at least in some, if not all, cases are addressed to the population of Samaria. Both of these give support to the conclusion that at a certain period, the two provinces enjoyed a fraternal relationship, to the extent of regarding themselves as members of a single family, worshipping the same ancestral god and sharing a common story of their origins. This is the 'Israel' of the Pentateuch.

The historicity of the Pentateuchal story, once hotly debated, is now of relatively little interest; what concerns us now is the origin and meaning of this story itself. If the current understanding that Israel and Judah had independent origins is correct, how was the name 'Israel' extended to include Judah, and its meaning transformed from a political to an ethnic/religious one? Was this twelve-tribe 'Israel' the product of a fiction deliberately created by a committee of Samarian and Judahite leaders to give a historical dimension to their brotherhood? Or was the bulk of the story already part of the collective memory of the kingdom of Israel? The answer to that question is more important to the modern historian than finding odd traces of historical fact in the Pentateuchal stories. For here we seem to have an 'Israel' that existed in no shared political form, with no shared land but only in a shared worship of the same deity and a belief that they belonged to the same people. In one sense, this 'Israel' is unhistorical; in another sense, as a belief that was once held and which governed the behaviour of people in Judah and Samaria, it *is* historical. And the Pentateuch is the historiography of this Israel.

Ezra–Nehemiah

Once Ezra–Nehemiah is detached from Chronicles, it appears in a quite different light as a piece of historiography. The common scholarly approach until recently has been to consider these books as historically reliable, and to focus on the problem of which of the characters arrived first and how their very similar duties overlapped, for each seems to be fulfilling an official leadership role at about the same time, yet they are mentioned together only in one place, Nehemiah 8. Otherwise, the name Nehemiah appears only once in Ezra, at 2.2, as a name in a list of returnees, and we cannot easily identify this person with the governor who is sent later in the book of Nehemiah. The name Ezra appears also five times in Nehemiah 12, always in a list except for v. 26, which includes the phrase 'in the days of Nehemiah the governor and of Ezra the priest-scribe'. This is an unlikely state of affairs if the two books were written by one author as a single story. The obvious conclusion is that we have here two quite independent stories, covering a similar period. The story of Nehemiah 8, where Ezra officiates, belongs better with the rest of the Ezra material, but has possibly been moved in order to bring the two stories together and connect both leaders with the crucial ceremony of renewal described in this chapter. Nehemiah 12.26 looks as if it may also be an editorial comment intended to confirm the impression that a single story is being told here.

This suggestion would partly explain why Ezra and Nehemiah comprise a single book in the Hebrew canon but two books in the Greek Old Testament (and hence in modern Christian Bibles). In looking at the two separately, several differences in structure and vocabulary further suggest that they are in fact independent compositions. Ezra's story begins only in Ezra 7, the preceding chapters being given over to a list of those who returned with Zerubbabel (Chs 1–2), and the resumption of the cult in Jerusalem, together with the commencement of temple-building. Opposition to this enterprise from other neighbouring leaders is described in Chapters 4–5 (where the names of Haggai and Zechariah appear also), along with letters to and from imperial officials, causing work on the rebuilding to cease. In Chapter 6 the Persian king Darius authorized work on the temple to continue. Ezra enters in the reign of Artaxerxes (at least fifty years later) at the beginning of Chapter

7, with imperial authority to finance the temple rebuilding, deliver a copy of the Law, and enforce it not only in Judah but throughout the satrapy of Beyond the River (which would include Samaria). The main historical problem here is the time gap between Chapters 6 and 7. If Darius authorized the temple rebuilding, why is it still incomplete half a century later? Perhaps the book of Ezra is in fact two stories place together to try and create a continuous account of events between the edict of Cyrus in the 530s BCE and the rededication of the temple in the middle of the fifth century, a hundred years later. Or perhaps Ezra's dating was original earlier but has been moved in order to make him a contemporary of Nehemiah?

Nehemiah's story also raises chronological problems. The book begins in the first person, but Chapters 8–12 are in the third person.[2] At the beginning of the book, dated to the reign of Artaxerxes,[2] Nehemiah hears that the survivors who escaped exile are in great trouble and the city wall of Jerusalem has been destroyed. But are we to believe that this was still news a century and a half after the event, and that the efforts of Zerubbabel, Haggai and Zechariah are discounted? Like Ezra, Nehemiah receives royal authority to go, in this case to restore Jerusalem. It is as if Nehemiah's story belongs to the very beginnings of a process of restoration and not much later. One further difficulty is in establishing when Jerusalem was reinstated as the provincial capital. Presumably not until the walls were rebuilt, with Mizpah having presumably been the capital of the province for a century and a half. But Mizpah is not mentioned anywhere in these books, as if Jerusalem had remained the capital city.

This is not the place to attempt historical reconstruction (see Edelman 2005 for an investigation of all these problems). But what kind of writing about the past do these stories represent, if not, as once thought, reliable contemporary accounts? A recent study by Wright (2004) sees Ezra–Nehemiah as the result of a process initiated by a first-person Nehemiah report, embellished by an account of rebuilding, and with much of the two parts of Ezra later created to furnish a prologue to Nehemiah's career – altogether seven strata of composition (see the table on p. 340). Whether or not such an elaborate reconstruction is achievable, this analysis establishes the development of Ezra-Nehemiah as an identity-building project, and the simpler analysis offered above likewise views Ezra and Nehemiah as founder-figures of the 'new Israel' represented by the return of descendants of deportees, the 'captivity of Israel' as Nehemiah describes them. As we find in the book of Daniel and in some of the Qumran scrolls, the sack of Jerusalem by Nebuchadrezzar marks the beginning of a new era, from which the countdown to the culmination of history begins. According to these sources, this whole period is a prolonged 'Exile', to be ended only by an eschatological intervention. But in the meantime, the two pillars of Israel's life, the temple-city and the Law, have been established. The historical context of Ezra-Nehemiah is perhaps to be set in the fourth or third century at the earliest, and perhaps even later, since the figure of Ezra is unknown in any later Jewish source before the first century CE (4 Ezra), while 2 Maccabees 1 (c. 100 BCE) attests some memories of Nehemiah that differ from the biblical book. In short, here we have a Judahite, or even possibly Jewish, story about the origins of its 'Israel'. We can call it 'Israel' because both Ezra and Nehemiah use 'Israel' to describe the body of people who are rebuilding Judah and Jerusalem and re-establishing law and covenant.

The biblical construction of the past

It is probably useful at this point to illuminate the nature of biblical historiography by focusing on three aspects of history writing that we nowadays regard as indispensable. One is an absolute chronology, in which every event and process can be exactly related to every other, and the distance between past and present measured. Second is a necessary respect for the 'facts of history', which constitute, in the view of most people, including historians, the raw materials from which every account of the past must be constructed. Third comes historical explanation in the form of some doctrine of causality, the thread by which individual facts become narrative and thus history that makes sense. Together these elements answer the when, what, how and why of the past.

Time

Our modern notion of time is linear and absolute, based on our modern calendars: we try to assign to each event the day, week and year in a system that potentially correlates every event anywhere. Now, in the book of Genesis we seem to be given precisely that. For every ancestor from Adam to Terah, we get a precise formula (e.g. Genesis 5, 9.28–9 and 11.10–26): the lifespan of each patriarch and his age on the birth of his primary descendant. Chronological reckoning continues into Exodus, but without the precise formula. But it looks as if two different reckonings may have been at play as the narrative was compiled.[3]

Is this reckoning based on actual records, or a long-established oral tradition? More likely it is the result of an overall chronological scheme. The clearest biblical example of how genealogies can represented a schematized system is in Matthew genealogy of Jesus:

> So all the generations from Abraham to David are fourteen generations; and from David to the deportation to Babylon, fourteen generations; and from the deportation to Babylon to the Messiah, fourteen generations.
>
> (Mt. 1.17)

Different schemes of periodizing are found in Daniel 2's succession of empires, each represented by a different metal, or the more precise scheme in Chapter 9, where the seventy years of exile given in Jeremiah is interpreted to mean seventy 'weeks of years', namely 490 years. The book of *Jubilees*, written in the late second or early first century BCE, divides the events from Creation to Sinai, into weeks and jubilees in such a way that the patriarchs follow the later Sinai laws (such as not travelling on Sabbaths). Is there a *canonical* chronological scheme?

Let us take the statement in 1 Samuel 13.1:

> Saul was a year old when he began to reign, and he reigned two years over Israel.

This is what the Hebrew text says. Most surviving Greek manuscripts, which go back to the earliest translations made of the original Hebrew, omit the verse entirely, while some of those that do include it make Saul thirty years old. The Syriac Peshitta (another fairly early translation of the Hebrew) has Saul's age as twenty-one. From this comparison it does look as if the statement in the Hebrew text is not simply a late textual error since later translations alter it differently. But if the length of Saul's reign is impossible, what about David and Solomon, each of whom reigned forty years? Is that really credible, or should we understand forty years as a well-known biblical approximation (in which case did the writers have no idea of the length of reign of these kings?)

These curiosities bring us to regnal dates in general. The author(s) of 2 Kings and Chronicles enumerate the lengths of reign (and sometime age of accession) of every king and so appear concerned to provide an overall chronology for the monarchic era. Additionally, 2 Kings furnishes synchronisms between the rulers of Judah and Israel. The presence of any approximate or incorrect figures would obviously undo the entire exercise. But there are plenty of these. Amaziah of Judah began to reign in the second year of Joash of Israel, and reigned for twenty-nine years (2 Kgs 14.1–2). But we are also told that Joash reigned sixteen years (2 Kgs 13.10), and was succeeded by Jeroboam II who reigned for forty-one years (2 Kgs 14.23). Hence Jeroboam will have come to throne in Amaziah's fifteenth year – as 2 Kgs 14.23 calculates. But Amaziah's son Azariah/Uzziah came to the throne in Jeroboam's twenty-seventh year (2 Kgs 15.10). This leaves a gap of twelve years (Jeroboam's fifteenth to twenty-seventh years) during which time no one apparently ruled in Judah. Again, Zimri is said to have reigned for seven days only, beginning in the twenty-seventh year of Asa of Judah (2 Kgs 16.15–29). But his successor, Omri, began in Asa's thirty-first year. If we now bring in external evidence and correlate the biblical data with Assyrian and Babylonian king-lists we find several discrepancies, such as (again, the example is from Barnes), the accession of Hezekiah. According to 2 Kings 18 his reign began before the fall of Samaria (721 BCE), but Sennacherib's invasion of Judah (701) is dated by his own account to Hezekiah's fourteenth year, implying that he was not on the throne until several years later.

What should we make of the fact that the total biblical figure for the kings of Judah is higher than those we can nowadays accurately reconstruct using Assyrian sources? Believing the biblical chronology to be correct, and in search of a solution, previous historians have suggested periods of co-regency between some monarchs and their successors, or a system (in Judah, at any rate) of counting the monarch's accession year, or different dating of the New Year differently in Judahite and Mesopotamian calendars. Of these, only co-regencies works, and it is easy since the length of the co-regency is calculated by measuring the discrepancy. But co-regencies are never mentioned in 2 Kings, and the argument is both hypothetical and circular. But surely, as Julius Wellhausen had already concluded, the figures are, at least overall, schematic. To see this we have to note that the biblical chronology of which these reigns are part gives a total of 430 years from the foundation of the Temple to its destruction, while 430 years is also the figure given in Exodus 12.40 for the sojourn in Egypt. If we add fifty years of Babylonian exile, we reach a total of 480 between the construction of the First and Second temples. This is the same figure as 1 Kgs 6.1 gives for the period between the Exodus and the building of the First (Solomonic) Temple. According to the biblical chronology of Exodus, it was in the 430th year of their stay in Egypt that the Israelites left (and in which the tabernacle, the prototype of the Temple, was built).

What is the point of such schematization? One apparent problem with the calculation above, however, is the fifty years allowed between the destruction of the First Temple and the building of the Second. More familiar is a figure for the exile of seventy years, as in Jeremiah 25.11-12; 29.10; Zechariah 7.5; 2 Chronicles 36.21; cf. Daniel 9.2. Do all parts of the Bible display the same chronological system? Ezra 1–3, however, puts the commencement of the building of the Second Temple in Cyrus's first year and thus may be working with a figure of 480 years from the building of the First Temple. A fifty-year Exile happens to be in accordance with the jubilee law of Leviticus 25, according to which alienated land reverts to its original owner in the jubilee (forty-ninth or fiftieth) year, so that those exiled were entitled to have their Judean properties restored from those to whom it had been given on their deportation after a period of fifty years. And where does the seventy-year period come from? Leviticus 26.35 and 2 Chronicles 36.21 comment that the removal of Judah's inhabitants by the Babylonians allowed the land to experience the sabbatical years it had not previously enjoyed. Leviticus does not give a figure, but Chronicles does: seventy years.

This implies a total period of neglect of the land of about 70 × 7 (490), which is as close as one can get to reconciling a total based on 12 and 40 with one based on 7 (480).

There seem, then, to be two Exiles of different lengths, one of fifty years, the other seventy. Indeed, they seem to have been combined in more than one place. According to Ezra 4.24, the immediate work on the Temple ceased and was not resumed until the 'second year of Darius', which would extend a fifty-year period to a seventy-year one. Is the curious case of the twice-built Second Temple in Ezra actually a (fictional) product of schematic chronology? And is Saul's one-year reign likewise the outcome of schematic chronology?

The issue here is about the historian taking the biblical chronology very seriously, at face value, and on its own terms. 'Seriously' does not mean 'literally', but attempting to grasp the meaning intended. We can finish this discussion with the following calculation (Thompson 1999: 73–5)

Flood	1656 (after Creation)
Abraham's birth	1946/8
Exodus	2666
Building of First Temple	3146
Destruction of First Temple	3576
Edict of Cyrus	–
Building of Second Temple	3626 (allowing 50 years from the destruction of the First Temple)

From the birth of Abraham to the building of the First Temple is exactly 1,200 years. More significantly, the Exodus occurs at a point (2666) that is two-thirds of 4,000. By adding the remaining 375 years we arrive – in our modern calculations – at 538 – 375 = 163 BCE, the date of the rededication of the temple by Judas Maccabee. Of course, this calculation implies that the framers of the chronology were aware of the accurate figure. So possibly the endpoint is the year of desecration (167), or even a date a little in the future, the date of the expected eschaton (the culmination of history), which so many Jewish writings of the Hasmonean period anticipate.[4] If so, the present Masoretic chronology dates from the second century BCE. The point of all the preceding discussion is this: if chronology is a backbone of our modern history, then it is also a backbone of the Bible's history – but in a different sense. Biblical dates and periods tend to be symbolic. The modern historian cannot use biblical chronology as a starting point for calculating precise dates. This is true of individual dates as well as of longer durations: the lifespans of the antediluvian ancestors are just as precise as those of the Israelite and Judean kings.

Facts

Facts may be sacred to the historian, but what about sacred facts? Even though, as mentioned earlier, the books of Kings and Chronicles have a lot of text in common, they contain some differences of fact. The best-known example is Chronicles' assertion that although Solomon actually had the Temple built, the architect was David. Another discrepancy is in the story of Hezekiah's Passover, which Chronicles describes, while 2 Kings 23.22 says of Josiah's Passover that no such Passover had been kept 'since the days of the judges'. There are other minor discrepancies of fact: the king known in 1 Kings as Abijam is called Abijah in Chronicles; in Kings he is a bad king, but in Chronicles a good one, while the evil king Manasseh of 2 Kings repents according to Chronicles.

Of course the historian would like to decide which of the contradictory accounts is correct, or more correct. But in the absence of any other evidence, most of these cannot be decided purely by comparing the accounts. Possibly a decision can be reached by examining the character of each narrator. Here the conventional scholarly view is that Chronicles is based on Kings, and was written two centuries or more later. If so, the Chronicler is rewriting an existing work, and discrepancies mean either that the writers had some historical sources not available to the writers of Kings or that they are changing data to suit their own way of looking at things, without any direct knowledge of what the data are based on. If, on the other hand, Kings is dependent on Chronicles or both on a common source, the same question arises. Did writers

of biblical historiography sometimes change facts? As explained in
the previous chapter, 'facts' are a tricky concept when dealing with
a process that entails mostly retelling a story handed down and not
analysing evidence. In storytelling form and meaning may be more
important than details, and many ancient historians can be shown
to have followed this principle. It is in this way that the past is
reconfigured and reinterpreted for successive generations. Indeed,
why issue a new story of the past unless it *is* different?

But how will a new and different version stand alongside the
earlier one? The modern historical mentality will want to know
which is correct or more correct, believing that facts are either facts
or not. But where 'the past' is rather a storyline than a catalogue
of facts, it can be rehearsed in different ways without raising such
questions of accuracy. Our contemporary media provide adequate
examples of how even today we live among conflicting versions of
facts, often without ever getting to the 'truth'. But do our media
not invent facts? And do people not believe them? And is such
belief not influenced by what we wish to be true?

Outside the Bible, the book of *Jubilees* (mentioned earlier)
is an example from the first century BCE of the biblical story
retold creatively. The historian Flavius Josephus's huge work of
Jewish history, the *Biblical Antiquities* likewise provides additional
detail, conversation, motivation, names for previously unnamed
characters, all of which he, *as a historian* feels entitled to do in
order to render his account fuller and more interesting. And here
is an excerpt from a rewriting of Genesis found among the Dead
Sea Scrolls in the *Genesis Apocryphon*. Here is how Abraham
tells the story of Sarai's recruitment into Pharaoh's harem (after
Genesis 12):

> When the king heard the words of Hyrcanus and his two
> companions, which they spoke unanimously, he desired her
> greatly and sent immediately for her. When he gazed on her he
> was struck by her beauty and took her as a wife. He wanted to
> kill me but Sarai said to the king, 'He is my brother,' so that I
> could benefit from her. I, Abram, was spared because of her,
> and was not killed. But I wept bitterly that night – both I and
> my nephew Lot, because Sarai had been forcibly taken from me.
> That night I prayed, beseeched and begged, and spoke in sorrow
> as my tears ran, 'Blessed are you, O God most high, my Lord,

for ever. For you are lord and master of all and rule over all the kings of the world, to judge them all. Now I place my grievance before you, my lord, against Pharaoh Zoan, king of Egypt ... during this night may he not be able to defile my wife ...'.

This version of events claims, like a lot of Jewish writing of the period, to originate with an authoritative figure of the past, and on this basis can justify any deviation or amplification from the scriptural account. This account, among other things, salvages Sarah's virtue and insists on Abraham's concern for the fate of his wife, both left in doubt in the Genesis account. This is a cultural feature of writing about the past from which we have no reason to think the biblical writers exempt.

In the case of Kings and Chronicles we have also to take account of a larger scope of rewriting of the story of the past. As mentioned already, the 'Deuteronomistic History' hypothesis is widely thought nowadays to have undergone two editions, each with a different meaning, the first optimistic, while the kingdom of Judah was still in existence, the second pessimistic, after its end. There are no extant copies of the hypothetical first edition, alas, and so we cannot know whether it included the cycle of prophetic legends associated with Elijah and Elisha or the 'Court History' in 2 Samuel 9–20 and 1 Kings 1–2. If, as Auld argues (1994) both Kings and Chronicles have independently expanded their common source, both of them show the past being rewritten creatively. The same phenomenon is even better demonstrated by the three Synoptic gospels, of which one has no birth stories of Jesus and the other two stories that agree on a few points (Bethlehem birth Nazareth residence, parental names, miraculous birth) but differ on others (reason for moving from Judah to Galilee, exact location of birth in Bethlehem). The Fourth Gospel even rewrites the date of the crucifixion and thus does not include a Last Supper. It does not matter whether we regard the gospels as historiography or not, because the manner of conceiving and exploiting the past is not genre-specific.

There is one feature of biblical historiography, however, that is of particular interest, namely the presentation of two versions of the same incident, with the effect of, on occasions, having the same event occur twice. In Genesis, the Creation of the world occurs twice, and with major differences, and also the account of the dispersal of the human race (Genesis 10 and 11). But on other occasions two variant accounts seem to have been integrated into a single one (the Flood story, for example, or the election of Saul of his first meeting with David). What we learn from this is that while it seemed preferable at times to condense a single version from two versions, sometimes it was preferable – and acceptable – to put two versions consecutively. The modern or literalistic reader may conclude that therefore the same event happened twice is a slightly different way, but the ancient reader may well have been a little more astute and understood that there was no way of knowing 'what had happened' and that two versions conveyed a fuller understanding than one. The modern historian would be wise to follow the historical way of reading and not the contemporary one!

Discrepancies can, however, reveal facets of history, not about the event narrated but the narration itself and the issues entailed in dealing with a particular event. An example is the question of which tribe possesses the city of Jerusalem:

> The people of Judah could not drive out the Jebusites, the inhabitants of Jerusalem; so the Jebusites live with the people of Judah in Jerusalem to this day.
>
> (Josh. 15.63)

> Zela, Haeleph, Jebus (that is, Jerusalem), Gibeah and Kiriath-jearim – fourteen towns with their villages. This is the inheritance of the tribe of Benjamin according to its families.
>
> (Josh. 18.28)

> Then the people of Judah fought against Jerusalem and took it. They put it to the sword and set the city on fire.
>
> (Judg. 1.8)

> But the Benjaminites did not drive out the Jebusites who lived in Jerusalem; so the Jebusites have lived in Jerusalem among the Benjaminites to this day.
>
> (Judg. 1.21)

> David took the head of the Philistine and brought it to Jerusalem; but he put his armour in his tent.
>
> (1 Sam. 17.54)

> The king and his men marched to Jerusalem against the
> Jebusites, the inhabitants of the land, who said to David, 'You
> will not come in here, even the blind and the lame will turn you
> back' – thinking, 'David cannot come in here.'
>
> (2 Sam. 5.6)

The biblical writers obviously have different ideas about how and
when the city came to be Judean and indeed whether it belonged
to Judah or Benjamin. Of course, explanations for this kind of
discrepancy can be given by assigning them to different periods or
editors. But the point is that these things are allowed to stand in the
text without resolution. The discrepancies either were not noticed
(which seems unlikely) or were not bothered about, or were left
as way of *not* resolving what may have been a bitter dispute
– leaving each side with a statement of its claims. The modern
historian needs to appreciate the ways in which biblical writers are
punctilious about their 'facts', which in turn reveals to just what
they thought they were doing with the past, and why.

Causality

The final backbone of modern history writing is explanation of
how and why things happen, what drives the story. Let us consider
three possibilities. One is coincidence, which is a common device in
fiction that allows the unexpected to tilt the plot and jolt the reader.
Another is human motivation; a third is divine direction.

A modern history would offer the following explanation of
the end of the kingdoms of Israel and Judah. From the ninth
century BCE onwards, the Assyrians embarked on an expansion
policy that led them towards the Mediterranean and threatened
the kingdoms of Syria and Palestine. The kingdom of Israel was
drawn into resisting this advance, but ended paying tribute and,
after withholding it (effectively rebelling), was dismantled and
reorganized into three Assyrian provinces. Judah was at first an ally
of Assyria (in return for tribute), and after a rebellion by Hezekiah
that was punished by the destruction of most of the country,
with Jerusalem and little else left, the kingdom was returned to
obedience and, under Manasseh, even willing subjection. This
account of the facts is based on combining what the books of

Kings tell us, what the Assyrian records tell us, what archaeology tells us and an understanding of how historical processes work – in this case conflicts of national interest in which the big power usually wins. Hence, we would nowadays argue, Assyria was poor in manpower and natural resources as well as landlocked. Its expansion was dictated partly by economic considerations. Its military superiority, which was partly a result of its political organization, explains its success. Sennacherib's devastation of Judah came about because Assyria was stronger, but Jerusalem was spared. The reasons for Hezekiah's rebellion probably involve the hope of assistance from Egypt, or perhaps a gamble on Assyria's distraction by resistance elsewhere. No ancient source tells us. But now we have an interesting question on which sources give us answers. The Assyrian king, according to two sources, was bought off with a huge payment, and as a result abandoned the siege because his objective – submission – had been achieved. In his annals the Assyrian king would ascribe some credit to the mighty god Asshur, too. The writers of Kings have quite different notions of causality. They are uninterested in economic factors or *Realpolitik*, though surely they were not entirely ignorant of these. They are uninterested, indeed, in human motivation. But they do believe that history has a global explanation: it is what God – *their* god – determines. This belief is not peculiar to biblical historians. Most ancient historians also accepted this, including Herodotus, though his gods were many and capricious. Thucydides was exceptional in denying divine causality and in this he comes closer to his modern counterparts than any of his contemporaries (and most of his successors). But in the biblical scheme only one god is involved, and this makes it special. History cannot be explained by conflicts between different gods, which was a common explanation for other ancient historians. And the god in question, if not always rational, but rather jealous, quick-tempered and quixotic, was both a national and a universal one with a fairly constant policy. The Assyrians (or at least their rulers) actually came quite close to this idea, along with the Achaemenid rulers of Persia who founded the empire. But they did not leave us any bibles, or any historiography, and so we cannot say whether the biblical understanding of history was unique. But in the Bible, the history of Israel and Judah (which the biblical historians represent as a single nation) is not just *part* of universal history but the focus of it. Assyria and Babylonia are pawns, manipulated to punish Israel and Judah for their infidelity to their god. Military superiority, territorial ambition, the usual pattern of relations between kings and kingdoms, is of no consequence (though it obviates the need for overt miracles in this case). However, by way of contradiction, these nations are nevertheless held responsible for their actions: despite following divine prompting, they nevertheless receive rebuke, and threat of divine punishment in their turn.

Similarly, when the 'families' of humanity spread across the world and develop different languages, it is either because of a divine act (the collapsing of the tower and city of Babel/Babylon) or just a matter of course (Genesis 10). When Terah leaves Ur, he has no reason; when Abram goes to Canaan, it is simply because he is told to by his god. The cause of nearly all things is divine initiative, and there is little curiosity about why most events occur. Social, political or economic motivation is rarely cited. The patriarchs go from time to time to Egypt, and they do so because of famine. But famines were caused by divine action (see Amos 4.6). The point is not that we should *expect* a pre-scientific culture to understand disease, economics, meteorology, or any of our modern explanations. Rather, we must allow that in respect of the third backbone of history, causality, biblical writers had a very different worldview from ours. History was not understood as a dynamic process.

So when the account in 2 Kings 18 of Sennacherib's siege of Jerusalem reports that the king consulted the prophet Isaiah who told him that God would 'put a spirit' in the Assyrian king so that he would hear a rumour causing him to return to this land, and then 'cause him to fall by the sword' there, and that later an 'angel of death' slew 185,000 of the Assyrian besiegers, we moderns are a little unsatisfied; these comments do not allow us to understand what was really going on. So we explain that, for instance, Sennacherib had to leave hurriedly to quash a rebellion; or, following a hint from a story in Herodotus, that mice gnawed through the leather of the Assyrian armour. But preserving the facts (whether legitimately or not) while jettisoning the explanation damages the integrity of the biblical account, because if God was not responsible, there is no point in history.

In much of what has just been described, the ancient writers follow the conventions of their time. In the Greek and its derived Latin historiography we can see, as well as the beginnings of

questioning of sources and of comparison of accounts, a gradual
waning of deference to divine motivation and a concentration
on human causation. But we nearly always find am embedded
morality. If in other respects the biblical historiography is less
critically developed, it is one and the same with its insistence that
if history does not teach something – and that means something to
the present and something for the future – it is not worth doing.
The modern historian is becoming more and more interested in
ancient mindsets, and in the case of the Bible, where the facts are
often impossible to establish, it is often more productive to pay
attention to the history that shows itself in ways of thinking and
writing about the past.

The relevance of the biblical prophets to history and historiography is a complex topic in itself, and deserves a fuller
treatment than it will receive here. There are two longer pieces
of historiographical narrative in Isaiah (36–9) and Jeremiah (52)
which are both also contained (with sight variations) in 2 Kings.
In addition, parts of other prophetic books contain accounts of
more or less public events (Haggai, Amos 7). All this material can
plausibly be connected with the same circles responsible for the
'Deuteronomistic' historiography, and indeed the introductions to
many of the prophetic books comprise the kind of regnal dating
that is found in the books of Kings. The stories of Samuel and Saul
and the tales of Elijah and Elisha also reinforce the role of prophecy
as a *political* institution alongside kingship. There seems to have
been an effort among the Judahite scribes to incorporate the
prophets into the history of Judah, as part of their overall understanding of the historical process itself, in which divine warnings
of the consequences of abandoning the god Yahweh were issued,
and, generally, ignored. Perhaps the close connection between the
writing of history and the institution of prophecy explains why
in the Hebrew canon the books of Joshua to Kings are entitled
'Former Prophets'.

In modern history writing, the prophets and prophecy have
also played a part. The assumption that the prophetic books relate
authentically the words of historical individuals addressed to their
contemporaries, but also foreseeing the future, was, until the
second half of the twentieth century, standard; and it was understood (even by Wellhausen) that 'prophetic religion' represented
the authentic voice of 'Israelite religion'. Hence the lives of the

prophets were featured within many modern *Histories of Israel*. But the relationship between the figures featured in the prophetic books and the books themselves has now become problematic. It was always known that the book of Isaiah, for example, contains material from later than the time ascribed to the prophet himself (Chapters 40–66), and that Jeremiah himself did not neces- sarily compose the long sermons, probably not even the famous 'Laments' or 'Confessions' in 11.18–12.6, 15.10–21, 17.14–18, 18.18–23 and 20.7–18, which express misgivings over the message he is to deliver, though these have long been interpreted as revealing the core of the prophet's character. The view that the link between the prophet and the book was through 'disciples' or 'schools' who preserved the message of the master has gradually come to be less persuasive, given the lack of sufficient evidence for them, and the weight of authorship has correspondingly moved further towards what were once called 'editors' but are now often regarded as the real authors of the books.

The crucial question for the historian is therefore how far the profiles of the prophets in their books can be taken as historical data and how far as ideological constructs from the time when these books were compiled or created. Put another way: do we relate the purpose (why written) and the 'message' (what is conveyed) of the prophetic book more to the contemporary audience of the prophet or to a later readership of the book? To say that an original 'message' can be edited in order to address later genera- tions is not exactly answering the question historically, because it simply assumes, rather than demonstrates, that the 'message' is authentically the product of the individual. But something of the process by which prophetic utterances come to be represented by prophetic scrolls can be plausibly reconstructed (see Davies 1996 for a fuller account) because we have collections of written oracles from prophets elsewhere in the Near East, notably from Mari in Syria and from Assyria. Pronouncements were usually made to or for the king, and these were either composed or transcribed for delivery, then archived. But no further editing work was performed and the individual prophets themselves attracted no biographical interest. This further step, creating *books* of prophecy, seems to have occurred only in Judah.

It does not seem unlikely that in most cases at any rate the prophetic books *do* contain a core of oracles connected with the name of a prophet, but perhaps written down rather than 'preached' and for royal or priestly rather than public use, then retained in a temple or royal archive. What prompted anyone to preserve them, elaborate them and create distinct collections, often with biographical details? What criteria determined which ('true') prophets were selected for such treatment and which ('false') prophets were discarded or discredited? What role do these books play in the development of Judahite religion and politics?

One possible answer is that they do indeed contribute towards the argument of the 'Deuteronomistic' historiography: that Israel sinned perpetually and was destroyed, while Judah also sinned but would not be destroyed, only punished. In other words, the issue is whether Samaria preserves a part of 'Israel'. This answer certainly makes some sense of the twelve 'Minor Prophets' that in the Hebrew canon form a single book. But Isaiah, Jeremiah and Ezekiel are quite unlike these other prophetic books and from each other. Each of the three 'major' collections is provided with quite a full historical context, which at least in the case of Isaiah and Jeremiah fits the content very plausibly. Both of these prophets have been radically recast by means of extensive addition, but the task of isolating what might be authentic to the original figure is probably worthwhile, and forms part of the historian's task. All three books focus in different ways upon a central triad of events reflections: the destruction of Jerusalem (Jeremiah), the deportations from it (Ezekiel) and Jerusalem's indestructability (Isaiah). Together these form a set of meditations on the acts of divine punishment and forgiveness that gave birth to the 'new Israel' of Judah and even to Samaria, and it is interesting that Samaria is not disinherited in Ezekiel, nor ignored in Jeremiah's oracles to the 'house of Israel'. But the perspective of all the prophetic books is in every case from beyond these events, looking back and making sense, and whatever may be discovered about the individuals themselves will not explain the creation of their books. But it can shed a great deal of light on the ideologies that shaped the writing down of the past.

PART TWO

'Israel'

5

Ancient Israel(s) in the Iron Age

'Ancient Israel'

Until recently, the biblical portraits of Israel were read as more or less the historically sound up to a certain point, and the agenda for writing a modern, critical history of this people seemed both simple and reasonable. There were disagreements about the 'point', and while, as has been explained, the premier biblical archaeologist William Albright and his followers took the story from Abraham onwards as a historical baseline, followed by Bright in his earlier editions, Noth and the German 'tradition-historians' regarded the story as far as the settlement as what ancient Israel believed about its past, but for Noth history proper began with the settlement in Canaan. Thereafter the history of 'ancient Israel' followed the biblical story through Saul, David and Solomon, and the two kingdoms. After the fall of Samaria history became confined to Judah, because the story of Samaria was not included in the biblical accounts. What the books of Kings say about Samaria was accepted: Noth (1958: 262) remarks of its population after 722 that the 'foreign elements brought their own way of life and above all their religions with them (cf. 2 Kings xvii, 29–31)'. He added, however, 'but with the passage of time they too were absorbed in the Israelite population left behind'. Of this 'Israel', however, nothing more is heard, as if it did not exist. It (or its leaders) feature in Ezra–Nehemiah as outsiders, as opponents of the wall-builders whose exploits are now featured as the next stage in the 'history of Israel'.

The modern historian's confidence in the biblical story thus extended to the claim that 'Israel' continued as Judah. To a certain extent, of course, this was understandable and even unavoidable, because of a lack of written and archaeological evidence of Samaria until the Greco-Roman period, when the 'Samaritans' come into view. But should the 'ancient Israel' of Samaria not also be fully acknowledged? The danger, otherwise, is of accepting that ancient Israel continued straightforwardly into Judaism alone. That perception is of course what Jews have understood for two millennia, and what remains the universal view. But it is not historically correct, as the remaining belief in the 'lost ten tribes' attests. For should these ever remerge with their identity intact from their long diaspora (which we can discount) they would not think of themselves as 'Jews' but as 'Israelites'. Moreover, if Noth is right in stating that the population of Samaria after 722 assumed the identity of 'Israel', then the modern Samaritans are right to insist that they are, if not the one true 'Israel', then as much 'Israel' as are the Jews among whom they rather precariously live. For the historian to recognize this other 'Israel' and its history is not to meddle in modern politics or to take sides with one or other community or religion, but simply to take the responsibility of writing objectively about all those to whom the label 'Israel' legitimately applies. On this matter alone, if 'biblical Israel' as a whole is an entity that transforms into Judaism, then this is not the whole truth about 'ancient Israel', and indeed the historian should be dealing with 'ancient Israels'.

But even 'biblical Israel' is not a unified concept. For the last fifty years, then, although 'Israel' and 'ancient Israel' continue in some quarters to be used unselfconsciously, historians are now aware that the concept has become highly problematic. The problem is not whether there continued an 'Israel' in Samaria after the fall of the kingdom, but on what basis Judah comes to be an 'Israel'. For while the Pentateuch describes an Israel of twelve tribes, including Judah, the books of Samuel and Kings describe two 'houses' and then two 'kingdoms', one of which bears the name 'Israel' and the other 'Judah'. And if, as now seems likely, the portrait of an Israel of twelve tribes attaches to an epoch upon which archaeology is now casting doubt, so that our story of 'ancient Israel' has to begin with life in Palestine, do we begin the story with 'Israel' or with 'Israel and Judah'?

If we look at the issue in this way, we can see why it is dangerous to define our 'ancient Israel' on the basis of the biblical story and then to employ that definition in evaluating archaeological or inscriptional evidence. We are better considering at the outset what we are able to infer about 'Israel' from non-biblical sources, and in the light of that to examine what we have seen to be biblical historiographies some of which emanate from Judah and some from Judah and Samaria together.

Archaeology and 'Israel'

A fuller account of archaeological history is presented in Chapter 7, but here we need to anticipate one important feature of that discussion. It is that, without literary sources, archaeology is dealing with nameless places and people. It can tell us what kind of places and people existed in a certain time and place but without something written it cannot identify them, and thus cannot generate what we have come to accept as a 'history'. Without the biblical texts, no ancient city would be identifiable, and without inscriptions it would be hard to interpret the evidence of building and destruction revealed by excavation and survey. A purely archaeological history of 'ancient Israel' is impossible because 'Israel' itself is not an archaeological datum, but an interpretation of data from texts. Where inscriptions have been recovered through archaeology, they also count as archaeological evidence, of course, but in this chapter we shall nevertheless review the two separately.

All Palestinian archaeology, including the climactic West Bank survey of the 1970s was, of course, furnished with an image of what it was looking for. It has never, unlike the archaeology in many other places, started with a clean sheet. The discovery of Iron Age I settlements in the highlands of central Palestine was immediately connected with the name 'Israelite', because it fitted the time and place where, according to the biblical story, the tribes of Israel settled and later established their kingdoms. It has been argued by some archaeologists that the absence of pig bones and the building of a special kind of dwelling, the 'four-roomed house', plus the use of a 'collared-rim' storage jar point to an Israelite ethnicity. But highland farmers of any kind would not be likely to rear pigs, and the four-roomed house is, in fact, not unique to this area or this time, while the collared-rim pottery is also found quite widely elsewhere. Even if it was, it would only point to a distinctive practice, and it is now widely accepted that ethnicity and material culture cannot be directly equated. The avoidance of pork as an 'Israelite' habit draws on biblical laws (of a later date); there is no purely archaeological basis for the connection, and the absence of pig bones has been noted outside the highland areas.

The term 'proto-Israelites', which is sometimes preferred to 'Israelites' as a name for these settlers, is less dogmatic but raises wider problems: do we call the Helvetic tribes 'proto-Swiss' or even the settlers of the highlands of Judah 'proto-Jewish'? While the historian might ask whether the population knew of themselves as 'Israel' it is unlikely that they called themselves 'proto-Israel'. To name a population on the basis of a name by which they would later be known is complicated by the fact that all sorts of people might have descendants who could assume that identity. Was Uriah the Hittite's grandfather also a 'proto-Israelite'? Many, if not most, of the people of Canaan who lived in the lowlands and in the cities and their inhabitants later formed the population of the kingdoms of Israel and Judah: does this make them all 'proto-Israelites' too? What we must beware of in attaching an 'Israelite' label is the influence of the biblical legend of the book of Joshua, according to which 'Canaanites' were replaced by 'Israelites' – and indeed, early Israeli archaeologists referred to the Bronze Age as the 'Canaanite' period and the Iron Age as the 'Israelite period'. But if the archaeologists must use the Bible, why select Joshua rather than Judges, which states that the Israelite tribes mostly did not replace the 'nations of Canaan' but lived alongside them, even sometime in subjugation to them – and indeed, following their practices? Following this lead makes it impossible for any plausible identifi-cation of 'proto-Israelites', unless 'Israelite' constitutes a distinctive and dominant element in the population. But archaeologically this is very difficult to determine: Philistines can be identified from their pottery, but not 'Israelites'. The material culture of the so-called 'Israelites' of the hill-country is indistinguishable from that of other Canaanites, and remains so throughout the Iron Age. And, as a final point, it cannot be archaeologically established that the Iron

I highland population all came from a single source. Behind the interest in identifying the Iron I hill-country population as 'Israelite' may lie a concern to sustain the claim of Jewish patrimony in Palestine from the beginning of the Iron Age, to assert a continuous identity throughout the first millennium and beyond. But whatever 'ethnic' identity may or may not have developed here before the political identity of 'Israelite' emerged, that is just as likely, if not more likely, to have been a result of living and interbreeding side by side and cooperating economically over two centuries, rather than having pre-existed the settlement.

A conclusion that the West Bank survey was able to draw, however, and which has been increasingly refined in numerous publications, is derived from an analysis of material remains, ecological analysis and architecture, that there was no single phase of settlement'. Rather, the northern highlands (later to be the territory of the kingdom of Israel) were settled earlier than that in the southern highlands (= Judah), and, moreover, that these two societies developed at different rates, not just economically, as would be expected from the advantages of the more northerly terrain, but also politically. The northern highlands have wider and more fertile valleys than to the south, and are also more accessible from other parts of the country. Given that the lifestyle of these populations was inevitably similar, it remains nevertheless questionable whether they regarded themselves as part of a single 'nation' or 'family' – or even, indeed, that they recognized each other as kinfolk any more (or less) than they both regarded the neighbouring populations of Ammon and Moab, which may not have had very different origins or early histories, and which the book of Genesis, for example, are related genealogically to 'Israel'. Maps of Palestine may give the impression of the Jordan valley as a natural boundary, but this is not actually the case.

Archaeologists therefore now need to speak of the 'archaeology of Judah' and the 'archaeology of Israel', even back to the beginnings of the Iron Age. And what of a kingdom including both Israel and Judah, that was ruled from Jerusalem? Many archaeologists still assume this to be historical and automatically relate their findings to the biblical characters of David and Solomon, two examples being Eilat Mazar in the case of what she identifies as 'David's palace' in Jerusalem, and Yosi Garfinkel in the case of Tell Qeiyafa (Mazar 2006; Garfinkel and Ganor 2008). But given the evidence of economic and political imbalance in favour of the northern highlands, how likely is this? The sparse remains from Iron I Jerusalem do not necessarily preclude the possibility of its functioning as a political centre, but hardly of a kingdom of the extent depicted in the Bible. To this the proposal should be added of a revised chronology of the Iron I-IIa transition (tenth century) that leaves little or no room for the realm of David and Solomon. But of course, archaeology cannot in any case verify the name of either king. But the invasion of the Egyptian Pharaoh Sheshonq in the mid-tenth century does not mention Jerusalem (or Judah) – although 1 Kings 14.25 has him coming there in the time of Rehoboam, Solomon's successor, and looting its treasure.

What archaeology is further contributing, too, is a more complex picture of early Iron Age political history that factors in the elements of the Late Bronze city state system that survived the collapse of the economic and political system at the end of the Late Bronze Age as well as sites in the Negev, the south of Judah, and the lowlands (Shephelah) that perhaps point to a number of local systems that predated the emergence of the kingdom of Israel in the ninth century. The undermining of the biblical and biblical-archaeological dichotomy of 'Israel' and 'Canaan' and the impression of one era and one population being abruptly replaced by another makes it precarious to speak unambiguously of an 'Israel' prior to the foundation of the kingdom of that name. For the archaeologist, as for the historian – necessarily relying on inscriptions – the only workable definition of 'early Israel' is as a political entity.

'Israel' in the eyes of contemporaries

What 'Israel' is 'referred to or reflected in the literature of other nations? Who else in the ancient world came into contact with an 'Israel' and what sort of an Israel was it? Here, too, the answer is largely the same: there is abundant evidence of a kingdom of Israel. But there is one other item that points us to the pre-monarchic era.

We begin therefore with the most famous and also perhaps the most problematic inscription. The pharaoh Merneptah/Merenptah at the end of the thirteenth century BCE erected a stele in Thebes commemorating his victories. The last few lines read:

The princes lie prostrate, saying 'peace'.

None raises his head among the Nine Bows

Tehenu destroyed, Hatti pacified

Canaan is plundered with every misery.

Ashkelon is taken, Gezer is captured

Yanoam has been made non-existent

Israel lies desolate; its seed is no more.

Hurru has become a widow for To-meri [Egypt].

All lands together have become peaceful

While the names of the cities of Ashkelon, Gezer and Yanoam are accompanied by a sign indicating a city, the hieroglyphs for 'Israel' employ signs denoting 'foreign', plus a plural marker. The context seems to locate this 'Israel' lies somewhere in Palestine, and hence constitutes a population living away from the city-states of the plains or the lowlands. This interpretation might fit quite well with some or all of the highland population identified in the West Bank survey who appeared at just about this time. But this depends on the dating of the beginning of Iron I; possibly the stele actually predates the evidence of highland settlement, in which case we still have the name 'Israel' but derived from elsewhere.

Nevertheless, for many, the stele furnishes a clear starting point for a history of 'ancient Israel'. Certainly, it represents the earliest record of the name, though the meaning and derivation of the name remain unclear. To take one interesting example, Lemaire (1973) considers that it derives from the name of a clan, Asriel, mentioned as 'sons of Asriel' in Numbers 26.31; Joshua 17.2 and 1 Chronicles 7.14, and in two ostraca from Samaria ostraca found in Ahab's palace and so probably dating to about 850 BCE (42.3 and 48), who were settled near the probable location of the city of Shiloh. This certainly raises the possibility that the name was attached to a group, but a group with an existing tribal or familial identity, from which the name of the kingdom was derived – perhaps even Omri's own family. This is, like all other suggestions, speculative, but then the equation of 'Israel' with the totality of the highland agricultural population, rather than a component, is also speculative. We do not know, and have no reason to assume, that the population of the highlands was originally homogeneous. The only firm knowledge we can draw from this reference is that the name 'Israel' did not originate with the kingdom, but was borrowed.

The inscriptions of the Assyrian kings are the fullest sources of information about a kingdom of Israel. The Assyrians first penetrated the eastern Mediterranean seaboard under Tigalth-Pileser I (1114–1076), but the earliest allusion to Israel does not occur until 350 years after Merneptah, in an inscription of Shalmaneser III (c. 853: the so-called 'Kurkh Stele') which inaugurates a series of such references. Shalmaneser refers to 'Ahab the Israelite' (*šr-il-la-a-a*'), accompanied by the denominative for land [*mat*]), and his 10,000 troops. So this 'Israel' is identified with a land, and a king, and while the name 'Israel' may have persisted from Merneptah's time there is no straightforward continuity of identity, since there will have been significant changes in population, social structure and culture. The kingdom referred to by Shalmaneser will have included parts of the lowlands (Shephelah), the Jezreel plain, Lower Galilee and parts of Transjordan, and so have incorporated other populations from beyond the highlands. The inscriptions do not tell us directly, but the participation of Israelite forces in anti-Assyrian coalition implies that the kingdom has probably come to be ruled by an urban elite, in which case it possessed a royal and a state cult, big urban temples, scribes, mercenaries and a developed administration. It should also have left us royal inscriptions, but the lack of any remains a puzzle (the two we shall encounter presently were created by non-Israelite kings). Israel's kingdom is probably very little different in character from the other recently founded kingdoms of Ammon or Moab or Aram, or others in Syria.

The remaining Assyrian references introduce a more common name for the kingdom of Israel: 'house of Omri'. Shalmaneser III's 'Black Obelisk' depicts Jehu 'son of Omri' is mentioned (and depicted). Adad-nirari III's expedition to Palestine in 803 (recorded in the Nimrud slab inscription) mentions Hatti-land, Amurru-land, Tyre, Sidon, *mat*Hu-um-ri (land of Omri), Edom, Philistia and Aram (not Judah). His 'Rimah Stele' introduces a third way of speaking about Israelite kings: 'Joash 'of Samaria', as does Tiglath-Pileser III (743–732), mentioning 'Menahem of Samaria' together with a list of other north Palestinian and Syrian kingdoms.[1] Finally, in the description of his conquest of the city of Samaria (in 722 BCE), Sargon II refers to 'the whole house of Omri'.

There are also two Palestinian inscriptions that refer to 'Israel' (in one case to 'Omri' also), which add details to the political and military fortunes of that kingdom, but nothing more about its nature. Since these also involve the question of Judah's status, we shall defer them to a later section of this chapter.

'Israel' as an ethnic designation

The question of Israelite ethnicity is not primarily a matter of 'when' but 'whether'. 'Ethnicity' is a slippery term, but one thing it implies is a consciousness of belonging to a distinct and separate social unit. Then as now, humans adopt multiple identities, national, familial, racial, but when are they aware of an *ethic* identity, whatever that is? Let us take the city of Dan, in what is now northern Israel, a town mentioned in the Bible as a temple city on northern boundary. But since boundaries in this time and place are not set by maps or determined by treaties, they fluctuate according to the fortunes of the kings and kingdoms that seek to enlarge them. By the ninth century, 'kingdom of Israel' means whatever territory is recognized as being under the control of the king of Israel, and an 'Israelite', at least to an outside like the Assyrian king, is anyone who pays taxes to that king. The Hebrew term *'erez yisrael*, 'land of Israel' is in fact used in the Bible only of territory comprising a *kingdom* of Israel, meaning that it would not have a fixed border (more importantly, it never includes Judah except for the reigns of David and Solomon, when, according to the sources, Judah was part of a single 'Israelite' kingdom [Davies 2013]). Now in the case of the citizens of Dan, we know that it was captured by a king of Damascus, who left an inscription there, in a language that has features of both what we know as Hebrew and Aramaic – in other words, the local dialect. After the conquest, the city was no longer in the 'land of Israel' and its inhabitants were politically speaking, Arameans. Did they nevertheless identify themselves as 'Israelite'? Or indeed, did they feel 'Aramean' even when they were paying taxes to the king of Israel in Samaria? Most probably they rather felt allegiance to their family and their city, both providing a stable foundation.

What might it mean to have an Israelite ethnicity, and when might that develop? As already said, it is not likely to have existed before the beginning of the Iron Age, though it may have been a clan or tribal name (and thus not 'ethnic'). If people from one or more areas settled in the highlands in the early Iron Age, they would have brought different identities. But if their circumstances require them to cooperate in tasks such as terracing and harvesting and the sharing of material culture, architecture and diet, and if they intermarry, a corporate identity could emerge. Whether, before the time when a political identity would emerge, a common name like 'Israel' would be adopted for a network of farming villages, we cannot know. A common material culture is to be expected, and with it common customs and habits, even memories, may have emerged. But once a king begins to rule and an organized state superimposes itself on a network of households, adding new networks as it expands, does any ethnic identity also expand, taking in other memories and customs originating elsewhere? Or does any ethnic identity disappear with the adoption of a political one, of subjection to a king? Or if an ethnic identity did not exist, would it now emerge, and if so, what would it express? Discussions of early Israelite ethnicity are largely unproductive given how little we know or how little we can with confidence reconstruct. More bluntly: the very existence of an 'Israelite' ethnicity before the monarchy is itself questionable, and the historian, who needs to decide at what point a 'history of ancient Israel' can begin, is advised not to be drawn into this beyond discussing the possibilities and conditions for extending a history beyond the beginnings of the kingdom of Israel. Ignoring the vast amount of scholarly literature on this will not bring any harm.

Judah

By contrast, a really important question (and one often ignored in discussion of Israelite ethnicity) is whether the land and people of Judah are to be included within the historical Israel. As far as a kingdom of Judah is concerned, there is no reference at all to either during the period of the kingdom of Israel before the end of the eighth century, after Judah had become an Assyrian client, when the Assyrian king Sennacherib mentions 'Hezekiah the Judahite' and both Esarhaddon (680–669) and Ashurbanipal (668–267) refer to his successor Manasseh. This fact invites several interpretations. One is that the Assyrians never engaged with the land of Judah or its king. A second interpretation is, then, that the Assyrians regarded Judah as a vassal kingdom, either of Israel or Aram, and too insignificant to mention. A third option is that there was until the eighth century no kingdom of Judah at all.

If we put to one side the biblical portrait of a kingdom of Judah going back to the days of David and focus only on contemporary inscriptional evidence, we have two important sources. One is the inscription of Mesha, king of Moab (c. 840), which celebrates his deliverance of Moab from the rule of Israel. He describes how 'Omri king of Israel oppressed Moab for a long time', as did his son. Mesha then relates that he recaptured the lost territories from the 'king of Israel'. 2 Kings 3 has a story that seems to be related to this reconquest: the king of Israel, here named as Jehoram, along with the king of Judah, Jehoshaphat, and an unnamed king of Edom unsuccessfully try to quash Mesha's rebellion.

Before consider further what Mesha implies about Judah, we should note the stele found at the site of the ancient city of Dan, mentioned earlier (for a comprehensive account, see Athas 2003). Dan seems to have been a border city over which the kingdoms of Israel and Aram fought for possession. The inscription, from the late ninth century BCE, commemorates the capture of the city by a king of Damascus after a battle with the 'king of Israel'. A group of letters *bytdwd* also occurs. It has been suggested that there is also a reference here to a 'king of the house of David' (*bet dawid*), namely a king of Judah. But the formula 'king' plus 'house of' never occurs in ancient Semitic inscriptions: Assyrian monarchs for example always refer either to 'house of Omri' or to 'king of Israel'. That leaves 'house of David', which might be the correct translation, though it is not as certain as some scholars claim. Following the publication of this inscription, 'house of David' was also identified in the Mesha inscription – which also contains a phrase *'r'l dwdh*, apparently containing the name 'David'. According to André Lemaire (1994) the latter part of line 31 reads: 'As for Horonen, there lived in it the house of [D]avid' (*bt [d]wd*). The reading is disputed here too, but if 'house of David' is proposed in two inscriptions we must investigate the possibility fully. And here emerges a very nice example of how investigation does not take place because the biblical texts determine the interpretation of non-biblical evidence. It is concluded that 'house of David' equates to 'kingdom of Judah', even though neither text uses 'king' or 'kingdom' and no kingdom of Judah is mentioned in any other inscription. By contrast, Mesha refers to 'house of Omri', and calls Omri 'king of Israel', while the Tel Dana stele contains the words 'king of Israel'. The references to Israel and Judah are both times unequal. Why?

What Mesha implies (if Lemaire's reading is correct) is that the 'house of David' was a client of the Omride king, having a ruler too weak to conquer or reconquer its neighbour Moab. It is striking that 2 Kings 3, possibly an account of this incident, while declaring the ruler of Judah a king (Jehoshaphat) who willingly agrees to support his neighbour, attributes to him the language of a client: 'I am with you, my people are your people, my horses are your horses.' All the evidence, such as it is, tells us that Judah was subordinate to Israel, and two inscriptions call its ruling family 'house of David.' We can ignore the claim that these references prove David to have existed, if by this is meant the character in the books of Samuel. But they might support the idea that the ruling house of Judah took its name from a 'David'. Whether the *dwd* was in fact a personal name is unlikely (no such name is found elsewhere), but this title might well provide the basis for the creation of an eponymous 'David' as the founder of the 'kingdom' of Judah. Here again, the historian cannot know, but can exercise responsibility by not being drawn into conclusions that are only conjectural. Both scenarios – that *bytdwd* explains 'David' and that David explains *bytdwd* – seem to have roughly equal plausibility. But the choice between them makes a big difference to how a history of Judah (and just possibly of Israel too) will be written.

So, while the evidence of contemporary inscriptions by neighbours and Assyrian invaders, supports the existence of a kingdom of Israel, whose capital city was Samaria and whose ruling dynasty was the 'house of Omri', none of these references predates the time of Omri and none sheds any light on the possibility of an 'Israel' that had once included Judah, but did not now. Whether there was a 'kingdom of Judah' is not the issue, however: this depends entirely on what we might mean by 'king'. No one outside Judah seems to have thought so, which might persuade the historian to follow. But an individual might claim the title of 'king' among his 'subjects' or a later chauvinistic historiographer might find it necessary to his story to have kings of Judah. What no ancient archaeological or epigraphic source explains is whether Judah ever claimed the identity of 'Israel' for itself, either in a religious, ethnic or political sense. The historian, again, has to decide how Judah is to be included in a history of ancient Israel', for clearly it does have to be included *at some point*, and the decision to be made is when this identity emerges, and what kind of an 'Israel' it is. It should now be obvious that terms such as 'southern' and 'northern kingdom' are now rather inappropriate, since they imply a kind of political unity of the two for which the evidence is still missing. Additionally, the historian has to consider whether in addition to a history of the Israel of post-monarchic Samaria, a separate 'history of Judah' needs to be written for the pre-monarchic period, and possibly a revised one for the monarchic period, too.

Summary: A history of political Israel

Political Israel – the kingdom of the 'house of Omri' – was a historical reality whose history remains to be clarified but whose outlines are clear. The evolution of the population of northern central Palestine into an organized state was not inevitable, but not unusual, either, and in the event of external pressure the emergence of leadership is a probable step. Philistine pressure can be inferred from their sites in the lowlands and in the former Egyptian garrison city of Bethshean. But several models of state formation (Frick 1985 is still a good resource) have been developed from anthropological research: in one of these the larger and more prosperous families and their heads emerge as leaders, who exercise patronage among other families. These organize defence and their ruler acquires the title and trappings of a king: the kingdom grows in size, territorially, demographically and bureaucratically. An alternative model suggests that protection is sought from some external armed group, and that the group comes to exercise a more permanent leadership (this models is actually illustrated in some of the biblical stories of the judges and even some of the David stories). The 'house of Omri' may not have been the first to call itself 'Israel' nor to attempt to create a kingdom, but we have too little evidence as yet on which to include any predecessor in a history (but see Finkelstein 2006a). This kingdom is typologically little different from the other territorially based kingdoms of Ammon or Moab or Aram or others in Syria, and, like nearly all of them, it succumbed to Assyria for reasons that have little to do with Israel and everything to do with Assyria.

As for Judah, much less can be inferred. There is no epigraphic or archaeological evidence from the Iron Age that the territory known as Judah (unlike 'Israel' the name seems to belong to the country and not the people) was populated by people that were recognized by others, as 'Israel'. Whether they saw themselves as art of 'Israel' and if so, in what sense, requires further argumentation that we shall look at in the next chapter.

This sketch is of course an interpretation of the evidence, not a set of scientific facts, and it is presented only to illustrate how far archaeological evidence and reasoning can take the historian and how much is supplied by the biblical stories, which, as we now have reason to believe, are not contemporary and in large measure are not accurate. What we *can* say is that there was an 'ancient Israel', and that it was nothing more nor less than the 'house of Omri'. Perhaps, as Finkelstein (2006b) has recently argued, there was a pre-Omride 'kingdom' in Benjaminite territory but archaeology cannot verify whether it bore the name of 'Israel' or had a leader called Saul.

6

The 'New Israels': The Post-monarchic Era

The biblical historiographies of the monarchic era end their stories with the fifth century BCE, while Ezra and Nehemiah tell a story of the fifth century. So these writings were composed, compiled or completed in the post-monarchic era. Their completion belongs to this era and comprises part of the social and intellectual history of the province of Judah, or at least part of the thinking of its rulers and their officials. It is from this perspective that they describe the past and this is the context in which they need to be analyzed. A useful start to such an analysis is to focus attention on the way they narrate the end of the monarchy and what follows it, for here we can perceive the relationship between the 'Israel' of the past that they portray and the 'Israel' of the present to which their authors belong.

We have sufficient evidence from biblical, archaeological and epigraphic sources to know how the kingdoms ended. In 722 BCE, Samaria fell to Sargon of Assyria, and the Assyrian province of Samerina (Samaria) occupied most of its former territory, but experienced considerable population exchange. Following the end of the Assyrian empire (Nineveh fell in 612), the western provinces were taken over by the Neo-Babylonian empire, against which the kingdom of Judah rebelled twice before also being reduced to a province (often referred to as Yehud, its Aramaic name). So the post-monarchic or provincial era began in Israel/Samaria over a century before Judah. After the end of the Judahite kingdom in

586 BCE, the Babylonians did not decide to amalgamate the two neighbouring provinces, but transferred the Judahite capital from the previous seat of the now deported royal and priestly elites to Mizpah, in the territory of Benjamin, which lay only a few kilometres from Jerusalem but close to the border with Samaria.

Both of the historiographies of the monarchic period (Samuel–Kings and Chronicles) take it for granted that the god Yhwh chose the house of David and the city of Jerusalem as the legitimate centre of his people's life in their land. As already explained, the writers present a single Davidic king ruling over respectively two joint kingdoms (Judah and Israel) or a single kingdom (Israel). Our information is that by the end of the fifth century Jerusalem was indeed again the capital and central sanctuary of Judah/Yehud, but the Samarians had built a temple on Mt Gerizim, just outside Shechem, which followed the same deity (Yhwh, the 'god of Israel') and modes of worship were as in Jerusalem. Political union between the two societies during the early provincial period, that is, until the advent of the Ptolemaic dynasty in the late fourth century, was out of the question, but there remained a sense of religious unity, though one divided into two cults. We do not know how far these cults recognized each other's validity, but while the Pentateuch acknowledges Shechem as an ancient Israelite sanctuary, omitting any mention of Jerusalem, the writers of both the monarchic historiographies imply that any temple other than Jerusalem was an offence against the god of Israel. Very probably this sentiment was reciprocated in Samaria and Gerizim, but we have no ancient Samarian historiography beyond the Pentateuch.[1]

The end of monarchy

The end of the kingdoms in 2 Kings

The historiography of Kings in particular looks back on a history of good and (mostly) bad kings leading their people from the principles enunciated in Deuteronomy, especially adherence to foreign gods. The kingdom of Israel is in this way derelict from the start, from the 'sin' of idolatry into which its founder, Jeroboam, led it. Judah, loyal to the 'house of David', experienced a series of similarly reprehensible kings, with the exception of just two: Hezekiah and Josiah. Its fate, however, is depicted as less conclusive than its neighbour's: it is the loss only of the land and not the destruction of the people.

Some interpreters have underlined what seems to be a promise of eternal Davidic monarchy in 2 Samuel 7, which, along with the notice at the end of 2 Kings of rehabilitation of the Judahite king at the Babylonian court, may hint at the hope of a kind of continuation of the Davidic line. Of course, it is also possible that this ending to the story of monarchy represents an absorption of native monarchic power into imperial power, a view that is expressed more overtly in Chronicles. At all events, the definitive end of the *people* of the kingdom of Israel restricts any future native king to Judah alone; and Judah is thus ready to become the people of the 'god of Israel', the 'people of Israel', as we find them called in Ezra and Nehemiah.

Kings does not explicitly name the people of Judah as belonging to a kingdom 'Israel'. How, then, does it configure the relationship between Judah and Israel in such a way as to anticipate the adoption of an Israelite identity that presumably its writers endorsed? The presentation of a parallel history of the two kingdoms, under the same god, clearly binds them, and thus expresses, implicitly, the notion of a single 'people', even though one that existed only in the past, before the final loss of the 'tribes of Israel'. There is also an interesting phrase, found in Judges, Samuel and Kings 'from Dan to Beersheba' (Judg. 20.1; 1 Sam. 3.20; 2 Sam. 3.10, 17.11, 24. 2,15; 1 Kgs 4.25) that allude to a kind of unification. But these texts all relate to a time when there *is* a unified 'Israel', of twelve tribes, and of one kingdom under David and Solomon: it does not recur once the two kingdoms are treated separately. In Chronicles (1 Chron. 21.2; 2 Chron. 30.5) such a phrase is of course natural enough, given the conception of Israel in these books. The fact that both Dan and Beersheba are also sites of influential (Yahwistic?) temples may suggest a cultic significance to the term, reinforcing the idea of a *religious* unity signified by a single temple of Yhwh in Jerusalem. At any rate, over even the separate kingdoms of Israel and Judah looms an implied greater 'Israel', the 'Israel' of twelve tribes fully apparent in the Pentateuch, though within the terms of the historiography of Samuel–Kings it is rather the unified kingdom achieved by David's occupation of two thrones. This unified kingdom is, at the time of Solomon, in 1 Kings 8 and 11, referred to as a single 'Israel', and, unlike either David or Rehoboam, Solomon is crowned only once (in Gibeon, perhaps because there is as yet no legitimate temple in Jerusalem). But this is anomalous and there are reasons to think that the portrayal of Solomon has been developed at a late stage when the careful distinction maintained elsewhere in these books between a joint and a single kingdom has been either ignored or deliberately suppressed. But viewing Solomon's kingdom as a single realm, a political incarnation of the Israel of the Pentateuch, enables the secession under Jeroboam, who takes 'ten tribes' (1 Kgs 11.31, 35), to be symbolized by the tearing of a garment; the logic of the narrative, however, is of nothing more than an ending of the union and a reversion to the status quo in 1 Samuel, where Judah and Israel are distinct 'houses'. Apart from this, 11.42 and 14.21 mention 'Jerusalem, the city that I have chosen out of all the tribes of Israel'. The wording here is very probably an allusion to Deuteronomy 12.5 (cf. v. 14): 'the place that Yhwh your God will choose out of all your tribes'. Deuteronomy nowhere mentions a particular place and indeed, as already mentioned, the Pentateuch nowhere refers to Jerusalem. But the claim is expressed here that the chosen residence of the 'god of Israel' is the capital city of Judah. Set as it is in the context of a separation of the ten tribes, the claim looks to be directed less at other Judahite sanctuaries than at the sanctuaries recorded as being established by Jeroboam at Dan and Bethel (which, as commented earlier, may be entailed in the phrase 'from Dan to Beersheba'), and that polemic may be a clue to a major purpose of the historiography: to establish Jerusalem's hegemony for *both* provinces.

The end of the kingdom of Israel is narrated in 2 Kings 17, which narrates that Yhwh was angry with Israel and removed it, leaving only the tribe of Judah (v. 18). Other populations were brought 'instead of the people of Israel' (v. 24). These did not follow the worship of Yhwh, for which reason Yhwh sent lions among them (v. 25), causing the king of Assyria to command a priest be brought back, who resided in Bethel and taught them reverence for Yhwh. Thereafter, according to vv. 33 and 41, the newcomers worshipped both Yhwh and their own gods 'as they do to this day', while according to v. 34 'they do not fear Yhwh and do not follow the statutes, or ordinances, or law, or commandments which Yhwh had commanded the children of Jacob, whom he named Israel'.

The explicit definition, or redefinition of 'Israel' here is a key stroke: the political Israel is now dead. 'Israel is now defined as the descendants of Jacob, and as the people of Yhwh, the god of not a kingdom of Israel but a people of Israel. From this account has arisen the notion of the 'lost tribes', the belief among Jews of later centuries that the 'Samaritans' were not part of this 'Israel', and the assertion that only one tribe (Judah) remained of the 'children of Jacob', which we may regard as the 'new Israel' by virtue of the change of definition into a religious entity. But there is some confusion within the account over whether the Samarians practised the cult of Yhwh or not. Most commentators resolve the contradiction – probably correctly – by concluding that the statement that they did not (17.34) is a later addition that betrays a hardening of attitudes towards the people of Samaria; previously it had been allowed that they did worship this deity, the deity shared with Judah (so vv. 32–3). We might conclude that in this chapter we see the crucial shift from an 'old Israel', represented by the kingdom of that name, to a 'new Israel' of which the kingdom has once been a part. But to gain this perception the historian has to understand the 'Israel' of the Pentateuch as the *new* Israel and not the old one. By a different kind of argumentation and analysis we would thus reach the conclusion arrived at by de Wette and Wellhausen that the Mosaic Israel stands at the beginning of the history of an 'Israel' of which the most influential and ultimately surviving embodiment is 'Judaism'.

There are other problems in the Kings account, too, and these might shed further light on how this transition from an 'old' to a 'new' Israel may have taken place historically. The mention of 'one tribe' omits to include Benjamin and Levi. This is especially interesting when the governance of the province of Judah had been, as far as we can tell, for the first century and a half of its existence, ruled by the Benjaminite aristocracy, presumably promoting Benjaminite forms of worship, sanctuaries and memories, including sanctuaries such as Bethel and Gibeon and memories of the great founding king Saul. In this connection it is interesting that Bethel is the place from which, according to 2 Kings 17, the Samarians learned the cult and customs of Yhwh. During the provincial period Bethel lay within Judah, and there are accordingly good grounds for concluding that it had always been regarded as part of the territory of Benjamin. When Benjamin's lands would have been transferred to Judah is unclear, but almost certainly not when 1 Kings 12 (vv. 21 and 23) implies that it did, namely under Rehoboam. The stories of bitter rivalry between Saul and David and their respective 'houses' make such a move narratively incomprehensible and historically most unlikely, given the military superiority of Israel over Judah and the claim of Judahite historiography that Bethel had been a royal sanctuary of the 'house of Omri'. In Genesis 28 Bethel is described as being founded by Jacob, who was then named 'Israel', and so this sanctuary may very well be regarded as the birthplace of the 'new' Israel, as well as of the 'old' one.

That Samaria was repopulated is true, but much else in the Kings account is suspect. Yet the story permits historical inferences concerning relations in Judah towards Benjamin and Samaria. This includes a recognition (one hard to deny) that Samarians continued the cult of Yhwh. Indeed, since the first half of the book of Jeremiah, which was completed under the auspices of the Jerusalem religious authorities, contains many oracles addressed to the 'house of Israel', we can perceive that this name continued to be used an recognized even within Judah, rather contradicting the Kings story, yet showing that there was no unanimity within Judah over the 'Israelite' identity of Samaria. Indeed, the modern historian needs to ask how it was that the variegated population of Samaria *did* preserve the identity and, apparently the cult and customs, of the former inhabitants. The story of 2 Kings account 17 may be impossible to accept as it stands (the lions, the touching concern of the king of Assyria), but the notion of priestly teaching as a means of promoting obedience to a set of customs is what the book of Deuteronomy seems to serve. Perhaps the story *does* reflect some such initiative in Samaria, and perhaps even accounts for the book of Deuteronomy, a possibility that will be explored in Chapter 9.

On the ending of the kingdom of Judah, the Kings account also calls for careful attention. It appears to state that all the inhabitants of Jerusalem were removed, and all the remainder save the 'poorest of the land' (2 Kgs 25.12). The implication is that there was no worthwhile remnant in Judah and that the history of 'Israel' would thus be carried on by deportees and migrate to Mesopotamia. The history of the land of Judah, until they returned, would be of little interest. We are given a brief account of the immediate disposition of affairs, with Gedaliah in charge (whether as governor or client king we are not actually told: the general assumption is the former).

After his assassination, 'all the people, great and small (i.e. old and young) and the captains of the forces, and came to Egypt, for they were afraid of the Chaldeans [Babylonians]'. The expanded version of this story in Jeremiah has the prophet among those taken there. We are not told what happened after that in Judah. The history of Judah continues in Babylonia (a lead that until recently was followed by modern historians).

The picture of an 'empty land' that the books of Kings leave us with has embedded itself in our consciousness. Of course it was not literally empty: no imperial king would deprive himself of income from agriculture nor leave the land at the mercy of invaders or immigrants. Currently there is dispute about just how poor and depopulated the land was (see further in Chapter 9); but this argument misses the point of the biblical story, which is that *no one who mattered* was left: the land was without the people to whom it had been promised, because that was the decreed punishment for their behaviour. We might well add the suspicion that since their beloved Jerusalem was also in ruins and without temple or royal court, the land was dead, and would only be resurrected when the city once more came to life. What would Judah be like without Jerusalem? Of course, empty. As Ezekiel put it, even Yhwh had left!

The end of the kingdoms in Chronicles

The ending of the Israelite and Judahite kingdoms (or more strictly, 'kingdom') according to Chronicles is more straightforward, but also internally inconsistent. Chronicles not only includes nothing of the internal affairs of the kingdom of Israel, but also neglects entirely to mention its destruction. We become aware of the fact only in the course of reading about Hezekiah's great Passover in Jerusalem: 'Hezekiah sent word to all Israel and Judah, and wrote letters also to Ephraim and Manasseh, that they should come to the house of Yhwh at Jerusalem, to keep the Passover to Yhwh the god of Israel' (2 Chron. 30.1). Later we are told (vv. 10–11) that 'the couriers went from city to city through the country of Ephraim and Manasseh, and as far as Zebulun; but they laughed them to scorn, and mocked them. Only a few from Asher, Manasseh, and Zebulun humbled themselves and came to Jerusalem'. Hence, in v. 25, 'the whole assembly of Judah, the priests and the Levites, and the whole assembly that came out of Israel, and the resident aliens who came out of the land of Israel, and the resident aliens who lived in Judah, rejoiced'. This latter group are explained earlier in 2 Chronicles 15.9, where king Asa 'gathered all Judah and Benjamin, and those from Ephraim, Manasseh, and Simeon who were residing as aliens with them, for great numbers had deserted to him from Israel when they saw that Yahweh his God was with him'. Thus the Chronicler has already prepared for the incorporation of the relic of Israel within Judah. It may be significant that the Chronicler speaks of 'Ephraim and Manasseh' rather than the territory of the ten tribes, because this covered specifically the extent of the province of Samaria, now perhaps tacitly rejected because of its refusal, while the presence of others from the 'land of Israel' (Samaria!) is a token of Judah's status as the future 'Israel'.

The end of Samaria is thus a non-event, literally, because unlike the authors of Kings, the Chronicler did not the unified kingdom of Israel survived: its capital and king were intact, and those Israelites who were left were part of that kingdom, if they chose to be so. They did not, and we may assume the Samarians contemporary with the Chroniclers were not interested in submitting to Jerusalem, either. They remain, then and now, potentially 'Israelites' if they submit to Jerusalem and thus join the 'new Israel' which, in the Chronicler's view, is an almost seamless continuation of the 'old'. Of the end of the kingdom of Judah, Chronicles is less explicit than Kings: '[the king of Babylon] took into exile in Babylon those who had escaped from the sword, and they became his slaves ... to fulfil the word of Yhwh by the mouth of Jeremiah, until the land had enjoyed its sabbaths' (2 Chron. 35.20–1). Although the image of an 'empty land' appears here too, the ideology of the 'exile' is different. The focus is on the land, not the people, who have been removed in order for the land to enjoy the Sabbaths (the fallow seventh years decreed in Deuteronomy and Leviticus) as it had not done during the monarchic era (the authors have therefore calculated this era as being about 490 years). At the end of that fallow period, the people would return, as indeed the end of Chronicles narrates, when the 'word of Yhwh by the mouth of Jeremiah' is fulfilled.

Yet this thesis has an interesting implication. If, according to Chronicles, the land promised to Israel and improperly treated includes the territory of the 'ten tribes', then that part has not 'enjoyed its sabbaths' and is not suitable for habitation by 'Israel'. Does the Chronicler regard only Judah as the land available for rehabitation by 'Israel', so that Samarians are only truly 'Israelites' when they come to Jerusalem? That would fit the overall ideology. It seems that the writers of both Kings and Chronicles have written off Samaria as part of the 'land of Israel', and regard the Pentateuchal 'Israel' as something that existed only in the past. Whatever the respective authors may have answered, each seems in some way to be trying to reconcile an ideal with a reality, namely that Judah and Samaria were separate polities with separate Yahwistic cults, and yet with (conflicting) claims about their possible fraternity. Certainly, both Samaria and Judah now represent different 'Israels'.

Reborn Israels

Kings and Chronicles

The transition from the monarchic to the post-monarchic era in the biblical historiographies of Joshua–Kings and Chronicles pose, as just explained, some interesting issues. For Kings the transition is ambiguous, for its final notice of the treatment of the Judahite king Jehoiachin can – as mentioned earlier – mean several things. But what seems clear is what can be recognized as a Deuteronomistic conception of historical causality at work. In addition to the remarks in Chapter 4, we can add that according to this conception, the futures of Israel and Judah are neither predetermined nor random but dictated by human behaviour, to the extent that it affects divine behaviour. Basically, adherence to the terms of the Deuteronomic agreement between god and people (the 'covenant') ensures the continued presence of 'Israel' in the land. But the causative chain also entails repentance, which can change the outcome, as it frequently does. At the point of Israel's destruction that is seen as no longer possible, but it is for Judah. The difference is imprinted on many of the books of the Prophets (Amos and Hosea especially). Hence, the books of Kings cannot end without leaving the future open. Those exiled are guilty but they or their descendants might repent and their history in 'the land' might continue. This logic is highlighted by the contrast with

Isaiah 40–55, and (see below) Ezra and Nehemiah, along with other texts where the exiled are a 'righteous remnant' (a very vivid contrast is effected in Amos 9, where the punished become the preserved within a few verses), and also with the third option of Ezekiel that Israel is restored for the sake of divine honour without Israel's merit.

In Chronicles, the question of a new beginning is, as we have seen, more straightforward. Chronicles ends (36.22–3) with an edict of the Persian king Cyrus:

> In the first year of King Cyrus of Persia, in fulfilment of the word of Yhwh spoken by Jeremiah, Yhwh stirred up the spirit of King Cyrus of Persia so that he sent a herald throughout all his kingdom and also declared in a written edict: 'Thus says King Cyrus of Persia: Yhwh, the god of heaven, has given me all the kingdoms of the earth, and he has charged me to build him a house at Jerusalem, which is in Judah. Whoever is among you of all his people, may Yhwh his God be with him! Let him go up'.

Here the author conveys a sense of recapitulation as well as continuation. The end of native monarchy is less of a rupture, since the 'house of David' of the Chronicler is the temple, and thus the rebuilding of the temple is a restoration of the status quo, with the difference that the figure of the king is now the foreign emperor. He speaks, nevertheless, in the name of Yhwh who has authorized him to rule. As Isaiah 45.1 puts it more directly, he is 'Yhwh's anointed [messiah]', the 'second David'. The exile of the Judahites, moreover, is not an end but an interlude, and the prospect of renewed occupation remains assured: the 'exile' was therefore predetermined to end at the specified time. In much the same way, the separation of the ten tribes under Jeroboam from Davidic rule had likewise been temporary rather than, as in Kings, leading to permanent loss. The books of Chronicles seem to reflect satisfaction with a theocracy governed by the priesthood of Jerusalem, comfortable with imperial rule, which is regarded as Yhwh's dispensation and thus affirming his status as the one high god. This stance lies not too far from that of the book of Daniel, in which sovereignty is assigned by the 'Most High' to one king and his kingdom after another, the difference being that Daniel envisages a final Judean kingdom. Whether either of the biblical historiographies of the monarchy actually implies a historical fulfilment of promises to Israel or to David such as the prophetic books often anticipate has to remain doubtful. They both rather seem to be engaged in defining the present in terms of the past, the primary role of any historian.

Ezra and Nehemiah

Until recently commentaries on these books on the whole took them as sober accounts of 'what really happened', accepting also their ideological stance, and focused their historical lens on which of the two characters, who appear to be doing much the same things at the same time, came first, why both were appointed by the Persian king, and what authority Ezra in fact had (since Nehemiah was the governor). It is only in the last few decades that the historicity of these books has begun to be seriously questioned.[2] The problem of the two almost identical missions has more recently, for example, been explained as arising from a combination of independent, even rival accounts of the beginnings of Second Temple Judaism, one featuring a priestly scribal figure mediating law and covenant, the other a lay city-founder.[3] On the historical existence of either figure, it is perhaps significant that Ezra is unmentioned by writers who should have known of him, like ben Sira (c. 200 BCE) and the author of 2 Maccabees, each of whom mentions Nehemiah. From the more recent perspective, Ezra and Nehemiah are founder figures whose profiles reflect the character of later definitions of 'Judaism' – that is, different 'Israels' *within* Judaism – and the historical context of these writings thus belongs later than the fifth century. How do these books (or this book, as it is in the Hebrew canon) define the 'Israel' whose story is being told?

The response to the royal edict to rebuild the temple to the 'god of Israel' in Jerusalem (Ezra 1) is made by 'the heads of families of Judah and Benjamin and the priests and levites'. 'Judah and Benjamin' recur in 4.1 and 10.9. Chapter 2 comprises a list of the 'people of the province' who came from the 'captivity of the exiles', and in v. 2 they are introduced as the 'men of the people of Israel', 'Israel' clearly being not a political definition but a collective name. The list concludes: 'all Israel' lived 'in their towns' (v. 70). In Ezra 6.16 the dedication of the temple is celebrated by 'the people of

Israel, the priests and the Levites, and the rest of the returned exiles' (cf. Neh. 8.17). What is unclear is whether the entire population consists of returners from Babylon or those already resident in the land are excluded. Nehemiah 13.3 ('When the people heard the law, they separated from Israel all those of foreign descent') does not entirely settle this. What can be said is that Judah and Benjamin (plus some from Levi) comprise the 'people of Israel', and that possible they are also those who returned. Of any whose forebears were not deported but were included we hear nothing.

The population of Samaria is defined quite negatively. As 'adversaries of Judah and Benjamin' they offer to help build the temple, on the grounds that they also worship the god of Israel and have done so 'since the days of Esarhaddon who brought us here'. After the offer is rejected, a letter is sent by their leaders to the Persian king (Ezra 4.9–10):

> Rehum the royal deputy, Shimshai the scribe, and the rest of their associates, the judges, the envoys, the officials, the Persians, the people of Erech, the Babylonians, the people of Susa, that is, the Elamites, and the rest of the nations whom the great and noble Osnappar deported and settled in the cities of Samaria and in the rest of the province Beyond the River

In Nehemiah 4.2 we meet Sanballat, 'the Horonite' who seems to be a leader in Samaria, and who, in concert with 'Tobiah the Ammonite', opposes the rebuilding of Jerusalem's walls. However, according to Nehemiah 13.4 'the priest Eliashib, who was appointed over the chambers of the house of our God, and who was related to Tobiah, preparing a room for him in the courts of the house of god', had a grandson who married the daughter of Sanballat the Horonite'.

Ezra–Nehemiah therefore reflects what has already been identified as a key issue in the province of Yehud and its writings: whether Samaria is a non-Israel, an ex-Israel or a potential Israel. That Samarians *claim* to be 'Israel' is acknowledged, but the population is characterized as foreign (exactly as in 2 Kgs 17). Yet intermarriage between leading figures in each province is mentioned in Nehemiah 13, which hints that this opinion was not unanimous. These books, without being explicit, imply that the 'Israelite' identity attaches not merely to Judahites only, but exclusively to those deported to Babylon and their descendants. We therefore have to reckon in Ezra–Nehemiah with the dawn of a debate to define not only *who* but *what* 'Israel' is within Judah itself, an argument over the 'true' Israel. In this argument – for example, in Daniel, in the non-canonized books of Enoch, in the Qumran library – the experience of exile and/or of the return from exile is definitive of this 'true Israel'. Once 'exile' has become an element of self-definition of the 'true' Israel, it becomes possible for deportees to claim a truer identity than those in Judah, and thus create another 'Israel', or for 'exile' to be redefined as a time of persecution, even within Judah. As we have seen, Kings, Chronicles and Ezra-Nehemiah all equate 'Israel' with those deported to Babylonia, with the result that somehow being 'Israel' requires an exilic pedigree. The claim that the history of 'Israel' passes from Judah to Babylon and back to Judah, and the coining of the 'exilic period' in so much modern historical writing has uncritically replicated this perspective, and the substitution of 'Neo-Babylonian period' for the years between c. 600 and c. 530 represents a more neutral designation for a long and important part of Judah's history, all the more important because of the way that the biblical texts decline to talk about it.

The 'Israel' of Samaria

Of the historiography of this 'Israel' we can obviously say much less than of Judah. It can be argued with some plausibility (see Fleming 2011) that the bulk of the Pentateuchal content comes from here, and we have established that Iron Age Israel is to be identified with the kingdom of the 'house of Omri'. But we have no other ancient Samarian historiography, which is unfortunate, because the gap permits and almost obliges the historian to reconstruct important developments in terms of what we know about Judah rather what we do not know about Samaria. For example, Second Isaiah is often credited with having laid the foundation of monotheism and Josiah with having established Deuteronomy. But such explanations do not explain why Samarians also had a similar cult of Yahweh, while the 'Israel' defined in Deuteronomy hardly fits monarchic Judah. It is unlikely that Samarians read Second Isaiah or obeyed the commands of Josiah! Perhaps, as Judah took the name of 'Israel' it also took a character that was created in Samaria, where the first of the 'new Israels' was born? Because Samaria experienced the loss of monarchy and a major change in population makeup, the requisites for redefining 'Israel' were more obviously and urgently present than in Judah. The modern historian must, despite the lack of data, accept the fact that there is an important historical Israel represented in Samaria and that, since the Judahite historiographies seem to be very much concerned with differentiating Judah from Israel while accepting some degree of fraternity, the history of Judah, and especially its 'Israelite' identity, cannot be explained without reference to Samaria. The birth of a Samarian 'Israel' from the kingdom of that name is more natural than an 'Israel' from Judah, but also a more remarkable achievement given the challenge of population transfer in much of its territory. In short, the challenge that faces us is to reconstruct a history that we know must be there and yet is largely unseen, rather like astrophysical 'dark matter' without which matter itself is inexplicable.

The 'people of Israel'

To some extent, the question of the Samarian 'Israel' is probably best approached through the fundamental question 'how did Judah come to regard itself as Israel?'. Five possible answers currently offer themselves. One is that there did exist at one time a unified kingdom bearing the name 'Israel', and that after its separation into two kingdoms, the common identity was preserved. There is no convincing evidence that such a kingdom existed, and several indications that it did not. A second possible answer is that Judah's period of vassalage to Israel resulted in a fusion of the two populations and their identities that persevered after vassalage ended. The evidence for that is in the second book of Kings, and it revolves around the identity of a king or kings named Jehoram or Joram in 2 Kings 1–8. Unfortunately, the sequence of events is interrupted by lengthy prophetic legends, which the authors of Kings presumably thought more important. According to 2 Kings 1.17, an Israelite king Jehoram succeeded Ahaziah 'in the second year of king Jehoram son of Jehoshaphat of Judah'. The sequence resumes in 2 Kings 3.1 where it is added that he reigned twelve years.

However, in 3.7 he joins forces with Jehoshaphat! This notice is generally taken to be a mistaken scribal identification: the stories of Elijah and Elisha are not at this point much concerned with royal identities, and commonly use 'king of Israel' and 'king of Judah'.

The royal sequence resumes again in 2 Kings 8.16: 'In the fifth year of King Joram son of Ahab of Israel, Jehoram son of King Jehoshaphat of Judah began to reign. He was thirty-two years old when he became king, and he reigned eight years in Jerusalem.' Now, Joram and Jehoram are variants of the same name; and hence two identically named kings are described as having ruled over Israel Judah at the same time. Moreover, the Judahite J(eh)oram is said to have been the son-in-law of Ahaziah of Israel through marriage to his sister Athaliah. Miller and Hayes (1986: 280–4) have proposed that Ahaziah was therefore succeed by this single J(eh)oram, who ruled both kingdoms until his death. If so, the circumstance has been deliberately obscured by the writers/editors of Kings by creating two figures, at the cost of some anomalies in the account – and in the parallel account in 2 Chronicles 21, which adds that Jehoram of Judah killed certain 'princes of Israel' as well as other sons of Jehoshaphat. This makes little sense unless he ruled both kingdoms. In any event, the account in 2 Kings has the Judahite Jehoram succeeded by his son Ahaziah (named after his grandfather). Azariah visited the Israelite Joram, recovering from wounds in battle, when Jehu had them both killed. Jehu succeeded Joram on the Israelite throne, while Ahaziah was succeeded by his mother, Athaliah; she in turn was killed six years later and replaced by J(eh)oash. The fact that Jehu is named as the son of Jehoshaphat, the name of the Judahite Jehoram's father and prede-cessor, might indicate further confusion on the part of the text's authors, and even imply that there was a longer period of shared occupancy between the thrones of Israel and Judah. At the very least, we are pointed here towards the possibility that whether or not a unified kingdom had existed earlier, there was some kind of political union in the ninth century between the two. Miller and Hayes do not propose that this led to Judah's adopting an Israelite identity, however, and the objection to such a proposal is that, having managed to free itself from absorption into Israel, would Judah wish to continue as if that absorption were permanent? One might rather expect a reassertion of Judahite identity.

A third possible answer has been championed by Finkelstein

(especially 2006b). His argument is based on two pieces of archae-ological evidence relating to the end of the eighth century, when the kingdom of Israel was ended by the Assyrians. The first piece of evidence is the quite sudden leap in the population of the city of Jerusalem at around the end of the eighth century or beginning of the seventh, which they date to two decades between 722, the year of the fall of Samaria, and 701, when the land was devastated by Sennacherib. The only event that they can therefore attribute such a sudden increase in population is the fall of Samaria itself, and a corresponding influx of refugees from the southern part of Samaria. Finkelstein's view is that up to half of the Judahite population in the late eighth/early seventh century BCE was of North Israelite origin (2006b: 266). But he admits that there is little in the material evidence to directly support the presence of such a new element.

This theory is buttressed by survey evidence that the number of sites in southern Samaria (between Shechem and Bethel) halved between the mid-eighth century and the fifth-fourth centuries, with an even greater population decrease. This might suggest that many of the population fled in fear of deportation, and that foreigners were settled instead. This last suggestion is illogical, since it would not result in such population decline! But the main thrust of the argument is that numerous Israelites entered Judah, and specifi-cally the Jerusalem area, after 722 and account for the sudden population rise there. Their arrival will also have brought, runs the theory, Israelite traditions and customs into Judah, and this would explain how it was that Judah acquired an 'Israelite' identity, to the extent of regarding itself as part of Israel. Finkelstein proposes that Hezekiah of Judah set about creating a new Judean-Israelite society, to which cult centralization made an important contribution.

That a significant population transfer really took place in parts of Samaria not to be doubted, though it is not at all a necessary explanation of Jerusalem's population growth. In the closing years of the eighth century Sennacherib devastated Judah and many refugees will have fled to Jerusalem. Thereafter Judah continued its integration into the Assyrian economic system and flourished economically. A combination of at least the three factors is most likely. But in any event, the suggestion that Judah took on the identity of Israel at this point is implausible, for three reasons. First, the conquest of the kingdom but the survival of Judah would hardly induce the survivor, an increasingly prosperous client of

Assyria, to assume the identity of a defeated neighbour. Second, the 'Israelite' identity assumed by Judah is not a political one. It is not the *kingdom* of Israel that Judah belongs to, but the *people* of Israel, a people defined by their allegiance to Yahweh, god of Israel. Given Jerusalem's escape from destruction by Sennacherib, a deliverance ascribed to the god of Jerusalem in Isaiah, it seems even less likely that the kings of Judah would feel any need to associate their deity with that of the vanquished neighbour. The third reason is the likelihood of both resentment in Judah against its more powerful neighbour, enemy of Judah's patron, Assyria, and also perhaps a degree of *Schadenfreude*, while on the side of Israelites, hostility towards Judah, or at least its kings, for having enabled Samaria's destruction by what could be seen as a treacherous shift of allegiance from Samaria and Damascus to Nineveh.

A fifth answer, which I have offered (Davies 2007), is that following the fall of Jerusalem in 586, with the loss of its royal house and temple and the transfer of political power to the Benjaminite aristocracy based in Mizpah, previously bitter relations between the two provinces began to heal, because Benjamin had once been part of Israel and its sanctuary, Bethel, had been a major royal temple. The cult of Yhwh of Hosts, previously in Jerusalem, was now amalgamated with the worship of the 'god of Israel' in the Benjaminite temples (especially Bethel), and became the official provincial cult of Judah, whose population thus became 'children of Israel'. This merging of identities will have been sustained for a century and a half, until the rebuilding of Jerusalem led to a revival of the old rivalry between the two and competing claims for supremacy within the cult of Yhwh. This rivalry led to the building of the Gerizim temple and the beginning of the rift between the Israels of Judah and Samaria. But by now the existence of the 'people of Israel' had been too firmly established to be undone, and hence the dispute was about legitimate claim to the name. This solution is the most consistent with the analysis of Judahite historiography represented in this book.

But none of the foregoing proposals has become established and it is unlikely that any of these answers will emerge victorious in the near future. Yet the question of how different and competing Israels emerged is central to any modern historical narrative and cannot be circumvented, for this is, in a way, the real 'history of ancient Israel', the history of a contested identity, that is needed to explain the production of the biblical writings themselves and thus to relate them to the political and social history of central Palestine in the first millennium. The historian must commit to one answer or another, and the answer must take into account the transformation of Israel from a political to a national-religious identity

Israel becomes Judaism

While 'biblical' or 'Old Testament' histories can legitimately end with Ezra, Nehemiah and perhaps Isaiah 40–66, most modern historians have felt that they could not stop with Ezra, perhaps seeing the necessity to secure the chronological link between 'ancient Israel' and the Judaism of the 'New Testament world'. For Wellhausen and many other Christian scholars, the deeds of Nehemiah and Ezra (especially the latter) marked a transition from 'Israelite religion' to 'Judaism', or from 'people' to 'church', inaugurating a long period of virtually changeless religious custom and belief brought to and end only by the arrival of Christianity. To be fair, a good deal of Jewish scholarship has also understood Ezra in a similar way as a 'second Moses', and the founder of a Mosaic religion that lasted until the end of the Temple cult and of the existence of Judah as a political entity. To those historians with a Christian perspective, the life and work of Jesus of Nazareth has often been understood in reaction to what was seen as 'legalistic' Judaism, and more in the spirit of the prophets who belonged mostly to the monarchic period. But at any rate, from both Jewish and Christian perspectives the history of 'ancient Israel' has tended to overlook the end of the monarchic period as one that inaugurated the transition from a historical kingdom of Israel into a set of religious 'Israels' of which Judaism was the most powerful and enduring and led to both Jewish and Christian religious systems of today.

Such a perspective means, nevertheless, attaching to a modern history of 'Israel' what is really a history of Judah, and ignoring the differences between 'old' and 'new' Israels. Historically, the Old Testament canon, the canon of Judah, achieves precisely this: of representing a 'people' from antiquity, which became divided and of which part was lost, leaving Judah as Israel, with or without the hope that perhaps the entre people might one day be restored by divine action. The power of the Judahite/Jewish canon, however, only came to be because in reality Judah's Israel *did* become the dominant Israel. How did this occur? During the Persian–Hellenistic period several communities existed, within Palestine, in Egypt and in Babylonia, that recognized themselves as 'Israelite', though in every case affiliated with either Judah or Samaria. In Egypt the affiliation was with Judah, and two Hellenistic historians writing about 300 BCE, Hecataeus of Abdera and Manetho, each write about the story of the escape of the 'Jews' from Egypt and their settlement in Judah (see Chapter 9 for a discussion of this). The existence of Israelites either in Egypt or later in Samaria is entirely ignored in these writers. This ignorance may be due to the fact that Egypt contained a large number of Judeans, for whom perhaps Samaria had now no place at all in the story of 'ancient Israel', though it may be more innocent. Yet here already it seems that Judah and Jerusalem are acquiring a regional influence that exceeds that of Samaria.

There is some evidence that during the fourth and third centuries BCE Judahites settled in other areas of Palestine, including Galilee and Transjordan (Knauf 2010). If this created a substantial Judahite (as distinct from 'Israelite') population, we may have an additional basis for the Judahite claims for Jerusalem as the cultic centre of the entire country reflected in the biblical historiographies. Additionally, we might consider a Judahite element within the 'Hebrews' (see below). Nevertheless, the decisive moment in the Judaizing of 'Israel' is the emergence of the Hasmonean kingdom in the late second century BCE. Under the Hasmoneans a political ambition manifested itself that, for all the religious issues and overtones, for all the religious rhetoric and the religious justification for the initial active resistance to religious interference from the Seleucid king, can still be understood as the result of opportunism and Judahite/Jewish nationalism. To say 'Israelite nationalism' would in any case be curious at this point, since 'Israel' was well established as a religious or ethnic or cultural term. But it is nevertheless possible to see how, once all the 'Israels' (of Samaria and Judah and their diasporas) had been taken into the political realm of the Jewish kingdom, 'Judaism' could refer in texts of this period *both* to the culture and ethnicity of Judah but also serve as the name for those whose inner religious identity is

'Israel' because of the absorption of members of the cult of Yahweh into the Hasmonean kingdom of Judah, and later the kingdom of Herod the Great (on Jewish nationalism see Mendels 1992; for an excellent analysis of the distinction between religious and political profiles of Judea, see Schwartz 2013). The succession from 'Israel' to Judah' attested by the Jewish scriptures is historically the outcome of not just the initial adoption of an Israelite identity at some point in the post-monarchic period, but the triumph of Judahite/Jewish nationalism in the second and first centuries BCE.

'Hebrews' as 'Israel'

Little has been said yet about Israels beyond the borders of Judah and Samaria. However, these too have a significant 'Israelite' identity, but with its own name. The common scholarly view has been that the name 'Hebrew' is a relic of the *habiru* or *'apiru*, mentioned in Late Bronze Age texts from Egypt, Syria and Mesopotamia as nomadic or semi-nomadic outlaws. In particular, letters from Palestinian city-state rulers to the pharaoh (the 'Amarna letters') refer to them as enemies of order. Sometimes they have even been identified with 'early Israelites' (see Greenberg 1955 for an overview), and in the book of Exodus this identification seems solid, though confined to Genesis 39–41 (the Joseph story) and Exodus 1–2, the story of Moses' birth. Most other biblical references are to a 'Hebrew slave' (Exod. 21.2; Deut. 18.12; Jer. 34.9). Otherwise 'Hebrew' seems to mean 'Israelite' also in Judith and 4 *Maccabees*, from the Greco-Roman period. Both Jonah (1.9) and Saul of Tarsus (Phil. 3.5) also refer to themselves as 'Hebrews', and so we could conclude that, whatever the historical and etymological origin of the word, it remained a synonym for an Israelite. But what kind of 'Israel'? A major obstacle to this conclusion is the naming of Abraham in Genesis 14.13 as 'the Hebrew', for Abraham is not an Israelite. He is clearly adopted as a religious ancestor, but the Pentateuchal definition of 'Israel' means Jacob and his descendants.

Another problem – which will turn out to be related – is that in the New Testament 'Hebrew' refers most often to a language, which, wherever it is transliterated, turns out to be Aramaic, not what we now term 'Hebrew'. In 4 Maccabees, where the 'Hebrew captives' are those refusing to eat 'defiling food' (in breach of the law of Moses), the mother of one speaks to her son 'in the Hebrew language', but whether here the meaning is the language of the scriptures or Aramaic, the vernacular of Palestine (and hence not Greek, the language of the ruler), we cannot tell. But we do know that the 'Hebrew' language generally meant Aramaic, and it would seem to follow that 'a Hebrew' was therefore an Aramaic speaker. This was true, of course, for Jews and Samarians, but also for many others, since Aramaic had been a *lingua franca* of the Levant, and even within Mesopotamia, since it was adopted as such in the Neo-Assyrian empire from the eighth century BCE. How could it, then, come to designate 'Jews'? The preceding section has explained how the Hasmonean kingdom, and later, Herod the Great's kingdom, embrace most of non-Greek Palestine, and thus 'Jew' would easily come to denote any non-Greek (Aramaic-speaking) native of Palestine. It is presumably in this sense that Saul of Tarsus calls himself a 'Hebrew of Hebrews' in Philippians 3.5; but why does Jonah use 'Hebrew' to identify his ethnicity to the sailors?

These questions bring us back to Abraham who, if not a Jew, could be retrospectively presented as one on a post-Hasmonean or Herodian definition, and in the light of this we may understand how Abraham comes to vie with Moses as the true originator of 'Judaism' in Greco-Roman era writings. This status is, in fact, precisely what is established in Genesis, where the patriarch is promised the land between the Euphrates and the Egyptian border – that is, Palestine – and even, through being the great-uncle of Ammon and Moab, parts of Transjordan. But only a very few scholars would date the book of Genesis to the Hasmonean period or later. We have to seek the 'Hebrew' identity rather earlier. This is made easier by the recognition that linguistically 'Hebrew' means Aramaic, and therefore a 'Hebrew' is an Aramaic speaker, and presumably a *native* Aramaic speaker. As the name 'Aramaic' betrays, the language has its home in Aram, Syria. Aram is also Abraham's homeland (where Haran is located), further identified as 'Paddan-Aram' (11 times in Genesis) as the patriarchal home from which Abraham's descendants (including Jacob) take their wives.[4] Abraham is an Aramean, and hence a 'Hebrew', and the etymology of 'Hebrew' can be made to fit. The name given by the Assyrians to the area 'beyond the Euphrates', which to them meant the western side, was, in Akkadian *ebernari*, in Aramaic *'abar nahara* and in Hebrew *'eber hanahar*, meaning 'Across the River'. This territory subsequently became the name of a Persian satrapy. A resident or native of this area could then be most easily identified as an *'ibri*.

The book of Genesis provides these *'ibrim*, including Judeans and Samarians, with a common ancestor. But in doing this it includes them within the orbit of the same god. The only explanation for such a pre-Hasmonean usage is that the territory was understood as substantially homogenous with regard to religion, as well as language, and, we may add, in the practice of circumcision too. According to 2 Kings 17.6 and 18.11 Israelites were deported to 'Halah and Habor, on the river of Gozan, and in the cities of the Medes, at the very core of the empire. No Assyrian sources state the destination of these deportees, though the identity of some of those resettled in Samaria is given in the annals of Sargon. But there is evidence that at least some Samarians were treated favourably and soldiers recruited into the Assyrian army. What we do not know is whether on the overthrow of Nineveh in 612, or the arrival of the Persians in the 530s, may have prompted any return to Palestine of those deported, whether their Assyrianization had been extensive or, by virtue of the large numbers of Aramaic speakers in the Assyria heartlands, some 'Hebrew' identity remained. But if there was no return of the kind that occurred in Judah, we have perhaps to reckon with a dispersion of a high god cult throughout Palestine, identified with Yahweh or a high god with other names, who could be represented as the god of Abraham, Isaac and Jacob.

If this reconstruction is correct (and even if not, the issue of pre-Israelite Yahweh worshippers in Genesis requires a historical explanation), then beyond the two Yahwistic provinces of Judah and Samaria and their cult-centres of Jerusalem and Gerizim (about a temple in Samaria we know nothing, but surely it existed) there was a penumbra that in the Jewish scriptures is embraced within the sacred history of the population which was viewed fraternally to the extent of extending special privileges to those who became slaves. It is perhaps not possible to write anything of the history of these 'Hebrews' but whether or not the Israel of Samaria had already embraced them, the Israel of Judaism eventually did, and so the equation 'Jew = Israel = Hebrew' was finally achieved.

PART THREE

Ancient History and the Social Sciences

7

Archaeology

Up to this point, historical investigation has gravitated towards the writing of narratives about the past and their interpretation, in which archaeology has played an important, but essentially supportive role. But what if archaeology itself were to provide the agenda for doing history, taking the literary evidence as subsidiary? How does archaeology generate history for other times and places, when there are no sources such as the biblical texts? What would happen if the same approach were applied to first millennium BCE Palestine?

The first thing to say is that archaeology is not ideally equipped for the writing of what the followers of the *Annales* school call a 'history of events', a short-term history of human deeds, of kings and wars and other political events. It illustrates much better the *longue durée*, long-terms processes of human habitation that describe the patterns of interaction between human societies and their physical environment. This approach to history will be mentioned in the next chapter, as representing a sociological approach to historiography, but it needs to be mentioned here in order to make the point that the archaeology of 'ancient Israel' has always been forced by the presence of the biblical writings and the huge investment in these writings in Western culture, to follow a course for which it is not ideally equipped and try to construct a short-term history of various societies that adopted the identity of 'Israel', despite the fact that such an identity is nowhere archaeologically visible. Thus, archaeology, even when its practitioners try to abandon their allegiance to the biblical templates, cannot do so:

it is still fixated on an 'Israelite' identity that may even have been alien to many of the people whose remains are being uncovered, because it has been bestowed upon them by others. Thus, it is not at all unfair to say that all archaeology of 'ancient Israel' is to some extent 'biblical archaeology'.

Traditional techniques

The history of archaeology in Israel has been told many times and there is no need to repeat it here (see Moorey 1981; Davis 2004; Cline 2009). Two important discoveries that permitted archaeology to generate its own historical agenda rather than to explore, survey and reveal, are the recognition of *tells* (Hebrew *tels*) or artificial mounds as the remains of ancient cities and the introduction of a method of dating by examining changes in pottery styles. The first of these we owe, in Palestine, to Flinders Petrie, though in fact it was Schliemann who first made this discovery at Hissarlik, the site of ancient Troy. The *tell* represents the accumulated layers of occupation and offers, crudely, a kind of vertical chronology, by which a history of the site's occupation can be reconstructed. Petrie is to be fully credited, however, with the second discovery, and 'ceramic chronology' has become the basis of archaeological dating. The principle is that at any given time, a certain range of pottery forms will be in circulation, and with the aid of careful excavation, meaning a reliable stratification of the successive layers of occupation, the evolution of pottery forms at that site can be determined. Note that it is the assemblage of pottery types, and not individual pieces, that matter. At any given time, a range of types will be present at any one site. With sufficient data from different sites, the typical life of any one type can be worked out. When the results are compared between tells, it becomes possible to correlate levels (strata) at one tell with another. The corpus of evidence has now accumulated to the point where the date of a particular stratum can be quickly determined. In theory the process is simple, but *tells* cannot be neatly sliced. The building of a new layer in a *tell* – which may happen suddenly in the case of destruction or organized rebuilding programme, but otherwise is a piecemeal process – may result in pottery being displaced to earlier layers, and it can also be reused in later ones. It is important to establish the position of any pottery relative to the floor of a building, for example, not only because buildings are extremely hard to date by other means but because the floors of building dictate the relative age of pottery immediately underneath or above them.

Because *tells* are not neatly stacked into horizontal layers, a system of excavating that does not simply try to peel off one layer after another is necessary. Large mounds are divided into areas, and within these and the use of shafts or trenches, developed in the mid-twentieth century, reveals the strata at each point and allows the stratification of a wider area to be established. Baulks, the walls of the trenches, also reveal changes in soil composition. Detailed plans of each area, stratigraphic recording, and the exact location of finds ensure that the excavation of a site, which destroys the evidence it interprets, leaves a record that will compensate for the fact that the remains are no longer as they were left. Finds are all recorded and photographed, and dirt washed through a sieve if miniscule remains are thought likely to be present. The development of CAD (computer aided design) programs now also enables sites to be reconstructed in three dimensions, leaving potentially a virtual record of the site at any point in its history.

If pottery is important in excavation, it is also the most common clue to the existence of ancient settlement where there is no *tell*, in which case the land is surveyed for surface remains. This must of course be done on foot, and nowadays in teams, but aerial photography, and now satellite imaging, can provide additional methods of identifying settlements, roads, previously cultivated fields and waterways. Magnetometers, conductivity meters and ground-penetrating radar can also be used for subsurface traces. Survey is increasingly important for determining the distribution and movement of human populations, which can reveal patterns of exchange and cultural influence. But, even more so than in a *tell*, preservation of surface remains is somewhat accidental and inferences must be carefully drawn. No single survey will discover everything, and lack of remains (which may turn up in a later survey) does not necessarily mean lack of settlement. But the accumulation of data from excavation and survey together can offer a picture of economic and even wider social activity within a region.

Culture

Modern archaeology is not all about pottery or buildings or *tells*. Trowels, buckets, brushes and bulldozers are not the only equipment. Botany, geology, petrographic and DNA analysis, involving a team of specialists, are also part of modern research, and several different questions are being asked of any site being excavated or surveyed. Ethnoarchaeology interprets material remains as evidence of social structures and religious beliefs, use of materials and technology. Funerary archaeology is an important element of this branch, because the manner of burial can be an important indicator of ethnic identity, and burial sites are often rich in well-preserved artefacts, including clothing and jewellery. Environmental archaeology examines the interaction between humans and their physical environment, enhanced by the study of pollen, seeds, animal bones and other relics of human habitation that illuminate everyday life, including technologies of tool-making, mining and hydrology. Pottery is no longer examined merely for its form (and thus its date), but the composition of the clay and the techniques used can betray much about economic interaction.

All this means that the recovery of objects (larger *features*, such as buildings or smaller *artefacts* such as pots or jewellery, or 'ecofacts', environmental remains) is not the goal of archaeology, as it once was, but a means to an end. Nor is that end merely the reconstruction of the history of a site or a region. It is equally to understand the life of the ancient occupants, and for this reason archaeology is generally understood (explicitly so in the USA) as a branch of anthropology, the study of the human race. Specifically, archaeology reveals the *material culture* of a particular population or society, and with increasing sophistication archaeologists now consider how raw materials were acquired, manufacturing processes and varieties of usage, patterns of disposal, agriculture, diet and cooking methods. From such analysis, it is argued, objects and their use can imply the beliefs and values of societies.

Dating

For the historian, nevertheless, the question of dating is important. History is a narrative of the past, and sequence is important! Various methods of scientific dating are now available, and the historian needs at least a basic understanding of both how they work and how they are reported.

Chemical dating is achieved by measuring nitrogen, fluorine or uranium levels in bones. Nitrogen, for example, decays over time, though the rate varies according to climatic conditions. The fluorine and uranium content increases over time, also variably. These methods are, however, insufficiently precise to deliver an absolute dating. *Tree-ring* dating (dendrochronology) is very reliable where trees add a ring every year, and with careful and multiple measurement, exact calendar years can sometimes be given, with the right kind of tree and in the right region.

Such dating is also used to calibrate *radiometric* dating, so-called because it relies upon the presence of a radioactive isotope in organic materials, the best-known being the isotope carbon-14 (^{14}C). A useful introduction to this technique and its application is Levy and Higham (2005), which contains several useful contributions to the major chronological issue of Iron Age Palestinian history, the Iron Age I–II transition problem (see below). The principle seems at first straightforward. Once the organism has died, the isotope decays at a regular rate. While a plant or animal is alive, it is exchanging carbon with its surroundings, so that the carbon it contains will have the same proportion of ^{14}C as the biosphere. Once it dies, it ceases to acquire ^{14}C, but the ^{14}C that it contains will continue to decay, and so the proportion of radiocarbon in its remains will gradually reduce. If you take a radioactive atom and wait for it to decay, the half-life is how long you would have to wait for there to be a 50 per cent chance that it will have decayed by a fixed amount, which has been calculated as 5,730 years. However, the calculation is not that simple. The level of ^{14}C in the biosphere has varied significantly and so the values have to be calibrated. This is necessary even for values obtained by the method of directly counting atoms, AMS=Accelerator Mass Spectometry. This calibration is done from a dendrochronological record of the ^{14}C age of these tree rings. This tree-ring record now extends back about 11,500 years, and by comparing the calendar age of the tree rings (i.e. basically a count of the rings) with their radiocarbon age, variations in the variations in the isotopic decay can be measured and calibration curves created, which will modify the bare results.

C-14 datings will then be reported in terms of probability, using the principle of 'standard deviation' (σ) that represents the amount by which the range deviates from the average. A standard deviation such as '2,000 +/– 200', means that there is a 66 per cent chance of the date lying between 2,200 and 1,800. Expressing this by two standard deviations (+/– 400) gives a 95 per cent certainty that the date lies between 2,800 and 2,000; three standard deviations delivers 99 per cent certainty but within a longer time frame. A single date would comprise a low probability and prove of less value than a series of dates from the same context, which may show a clustering around a smaller range. If Bayesian analysis is applied (a statistical operation of some complexity that refines probability calculation), a more sophisticated assessment of probability can be achieved. The reporting of radiometric dates is therefore not as straightforward as popular belief sometimes holds it to be, and without a considerable aptitude for mathematics the archaeologists (let alone the historian) will have to take the reporting on trust.

There are other forms of radiometric dating that need not be explained here, such as *thermoluminescence*, which works with pottery but is less precise than radiocarbon. It is a reasonable prediction that further methods of scientific absolute dating are likely to enable the historian to determine chronology more precisely, so that chronology may become a scientific field. For the present, however, there is still a degree of uncertainty and variation of interpretation.

Process

No less than with history, archaeology has its own evolving theoretical infrastructure, which broadly reflects a shift from ethnology and history towards anthropology. The 'New Archaeology' (or 'Processual Archaeology') of the 1960s sought to explain human behaviour in terms of societies as systems, and to search for rules that governed these systems. Thus, change was explained by the adaptation of these systems to the natural environment. Perhaps inevitably, processual archaeology has been challenged (by 'post-processual archaeology') as being too positivistic in its claims to objective description and its development of rules that supposedly govern human social behaviour. Post-processual approaches emphasize the possibility of human freedom rather than the determinism of behaviour that rules and systems imply, but there is no single post-processual approach. However, this attitude is music to the ears of historians who leave a great deal of room in their reconstructions for human initiative, including the impact of outstanding individuals.

The particular relevance of these issues to the history of ancient Palestine is in understanding change, especially the breakdown of the city-state systems of the Late Bronze Age, the emergence of autonomous communities, then the growth of territorial monarchic states and the growth of imperial systems that spanned the Iron Age. The period covered by the biblical historiographies is one of almost constant change, and the challenge is to explain it.

Ethnicity

The archaeology of ethnicity is difficult to determine from material remains, though in the case of ancient Palestine there is enormous interest in attempting to do so. The modern use of 'ethnic' is rather confused and it is therefore important to establish just how it may be precisely applied. As archaeologists use the term, it does not mean 'race'. Rather, it is a social category, and an *ethnos* may be defined as a group of people who are populating a given territory, who exhibit relatively stable linguistic and cultural traits, recognize themselves as different from other groups and express this identity in a particular name. There may be a common descent (*ethne* frequently express their unity by means of claiming a common ancestor), and may possess a common myth of origin. Beliefs and customs will be mostly uniform but not necessarily distinct from those of others. In the case of 'early Israel' a number of features of material culture have been claimed as indicating 'Israelite' ethnicity, such as absence of pig bones, construction of four-roomed houses or the production of distinctive types of pottery. But such features can equally be explained either as a response to the environment (pigs are more suitable for the lowland areas of Palestine than the highlands), or they are not exclusive to the highlands (four-roomed houses, collar-rim jars). In any case, the notion that ethnicity can be neatly aligned with a set of cultural practices is questionable.

Sian Jones (1997) has shown how the construction of ethnicities functions as an aspect of nationalism, which 'frequently involves the projection of an unchanging, essentialist culture and identity deep into the past in an attempt to establish the national community as "so 'natural' as to require no other definition than self-assertion"' (p. 136).[1] Jones does not refer at all to the case of Israel but her comments fit very well, especially with regard to the way in which archaeology is summoned in support of constructed ethnicity. But the concept of 'ethnicity' itself is a modern construct. *Ethnos* was certainly used in the Greek world but that world, rather like today's, was highly diasporic and colonial, with societies expressing a link to cities and countries from which they claimed origin or affinity while largely following the material culture of their geographic home. A sense of ethnicity emerged only in certain conditions: in one's homeland, one knows who one is. Thus, we can conclude, archaeology cannot tell us whether it is dealing with 'ancient Israelites' unless there is evidence (which must be literary) that the people used that name to express a common identity. It is for this reason that the historian should begin to speak of 'Israelites' in a political sense. But even here the population of the kingdom of Israel did not necessarily embrace a sense of ethnicity as 'Israelite' rather than as clients of the king of Israel, whose makeup varied with the expansion and contraction of that kingdom. A more productive way of studying 'Israelite' ethnicity has been demonstrated by Sparks (1998), who (rightly) eschews an archaeological approach in favour of an analysis of a range of biblical texts, aiming to reconstruct what is not a single overarching sense of ethnic identity but a set of identities that develops under different influences. There are, of course, problems both in dating the text reliably and in assessing how far these reflect a historical consciousness rather than an identity constructed by the elite responsible for the literature. But Sparks's study does emphasize one of the key lessons of this *Guide*, which is that many historical issues cannot be determined by archaeology, but require a sophisticated interpretation of literary texts.

Constructing an archaeological history: Israelite origins

Having explained how archaeological stories of the past are of a different kind than a conventional history developed from written texts, let us review what is perhaps at present the major archaeological debate, which concerns chronology. We begin by reminding ourselves that the archaeology of pre-classical times does not directly address absolute calendrical datings, but divides the past sequences into periods that reflect observable cultural developments. Broadly, these are Stone, Bronze and Iron Ages (which are global divisions, but appear at different times in different parts of the world), all of these being further divided into Palaeolithic and Neolithic (Pottery and Pre-Pottery), Early, Middle and Late Bronze and, for the Iron Age, in Palestine, Iron I and II. All of these periods are also further subdivided. The naming of the Iron Age subdivisions also varies from one archaeologist to another and the historian must be aware of this when constructing any chronology. The relative dating of these successive periods becomes problematic only when it becomes necessary or desirable to correlate the archaeological record with discrete historical events that entail a precise calendrical date, in our own case the biblical texts or related inscriptions. Understandably, but nonetheless unfortunately, the literary periodization of the biblical stories colonized archaeological interpretation from the outset. In modern Israel the Bronze Age was previously referred to as the 'Canaanite period' and the Iron Age as the 'Israelite period; 'biblical archaeologists' regularly alluded to the 'patriarchal age' or the 'conquest', the 'Judges period' or the 'United Monarchy' and the data were inevitably understood in relation to the character given to this period. This procedure has been quite dramatically revised in recent decades, but has not disappeared, since biblical archaeology, largely abandoned by academic archaeologists, remains dominant in amateur and popular discussion. To use a simple metaphor, while academic archaeology is now building a jigsaw without the aid of a picture on the cover of the box, realizing that the picture they are putting together is uncertain and even misleading, some popular archaeology is still trying to shuffle the pieces to fit the picture on the box. If we have become used to reading or hearing of sensational finds, especially when issued as a media event rather than in a scholarly publication where all the data are presented and explained, we must learn to ignore such circuses.

Another important feature of archaeological historical reconstruction is that it is a cumulative, even incremental exercise. Not only is this evident in the way that excavation is conducted, with maximal data recording for later analysis, and the assembling of pottery repertoires for sites, and then regions. It is also the comparison of results from different sites that gradually builds up the picture of social and cultural evolution. Moreover, since excavation, survey and analysis are now being conducted at a quite rapid rate, the jigsaw is constantly being rearranged as new pieces are being added and the existing parts are recombined into different configurations. Several elements are becoming clear, but the overall picture is emerging only slowly, and is continually open to contradiction or refinement. But because central Palestine is the most intensively excavated and surveyed piece of territory on the earth, the accumulation, analysis and comparison of data is becoming sufficient to put together a quite detailed archaeological picture of the Iron Age that can serve the historian. However, the story is quite different from the biblical one. The ceaseless publication of articles on Iron I–II chronology in particular means that it is hopeless to offer any extensive bibliography and in any case unlikely that any but the specialist will be able to keep pace. For a good discussion of the issues (and bibliography) see Grabbe 2010.

Can archaeology identify an 'Israel' at all? As we have seen earlier, the Late Bronze system of city-states underwent a collapse, and new forms of organization emerged in the Iron Age; this process is visible from the archaeological remains. But the farming settlements of the central highlands, from which, at the end of Iron I, small regional states begin to be formed, give no clear idea of the origin of their inhabitants. Several cities also survived, others recovered quickly, new cities emerged and rural life remained much as before. The symbiosis of city and countryside persisted, and these highlands settlements were not necessarily economically or culturally isolated. In other words, the archaeologist does not see here a vital or dramatic moment in Palestine's history when everything changes as 'Israel' enters the scene. The 'rhythms of time' as Whitelam (2013) puts it, beat on and on. As argued earlier, although one of the kingdoms to emerge in Iron II bears the names 'Israel' and 'house of Omri', we know this only from literary sources. What archaeology reveals is the contours of a regionally powerful kingdom with a capital city that could probably be identified with some probability, but not certainty, as Samaria. As far as cultural distinctiveness goes, the books of Judges and Kings repeatedly state that the Israelites and Judahites constantly adopted 'Canaanite' customs and the archaeologist would endorse that diagnosis.

The 'Iron age I–II transition' is the archaeological equivalent of the 'United Monarchy' ruled from Jerusalem, but neither David nor Solomon exists outside the biblical texts, and it is not at all clear that without the literary portrait any archaeologist would be able to infer such figures. That a single kingdom in central Palestine can be inferred at this time is unlikely, and the existence of a kingdom of the biblical dimensions is definitely out of the question. Few archaeologists seem willing to suggest that these kings and their kingdoms did not exist, but to be entirely honest that cannot say whether they would have come to this conclusion in ignorance of the Bible. These things are not *archaeologically* known, despite what some proponents may say.

The Iron I–IIA transition debate

The Iron Age extends from about 1250 to the advent of Persian rule in Palestine in the sixth century (though this is not everyone's calculation), and the most controversial part of this period is the transition between Iron I and II (or, more precisely I and IIa) is now the subject of very strong disagreement. This transition is characterized by, among other things, the emergence of territorial states in central Palestine, that is, extended territories and not a larger number of city-based states as in the Late Bronze period. When exactly did this occur? Before rehearsing the debate (which will have to be undertaken quite briefly), it may be helpful to state the three alternative chronologies. The conventional date of 1000 BCE

is now referred to as the 'high chronology', the 'low chronology',
initially proposed and championed by Israel Finkelstein places
the date about a century later, and the 'modified conventional
chronology' now suggested by Amihai Mazar, which has largely
but not entirely replaced the old 'high' chronology, fits halfway
between them. Fifty years or so may not seem a great time span,
but it is crucial if it coincides with the period assigned to the reign
of David.

Conventional chronology	Low chronology	Modified conventional chronology
Iron IA 1200–1140/30	1200–1140/30	1200–1140/30
Iron IB 1150–1000	1130–920/900	1140/30–980
Iron IIA 1000–900/925	920/900–800/780	980–830
Iron IIB 900/925–732/700	780–732/701	830–732/701

Source: Lee, Ramsey and Mazar 2013: 731.

The conventional ('high') chronology was originally achieved by
fixing the dates of David and Solomon through working back from
the reigns of monarchs in the books of Kings (including 40 years
each for David and Solomon), resulting in a date of around 1000
BCE for the beginning of David's reign. The transition between Iron
I and Iron II was thus attributed to David's defeat of the Philistines
and ruler over most if not all of the land. The next step was to find
archaeological data supporting this calculation. Two sets came
into play: one is Philistine pottery, the other the appearance of
monumental structures at sites in central-northern Palestine, and
especially Megiddo.

We now come to an illustration of how much archaeological deduction resembles a jigsaw without a picture. Philistine
pottery can be divided into two kinds: monochrome (Mycenaean
IIIC), which is both imported and local, and bichrome (red and
black), which is local and derived from it. Evidence from three
Philistine cities, Ashdod, Ekron and Ashkelon, led to the dating of

monochrome between the expulsion of the 'Sea People' (which we roughly equate with 'Philistines', though this is too simplistic) from Egypt by Rameses III in 1175 and their settlement in Palestine, and the subsequent withdrawal of the Egyptians from Palestine in about 1140, leaving their forts in Philistine control. Bichrome ware was thought to begin in the late twelfth century and to end in about 1000 BCE, fitting the theory of Davidic conquest of the Philistines. But Egyptian and Philistine pottery is never found together in any site, while monochrome ware now seems to have begun only after 1140, suggesting that bichrome pottery is even later. The evidence probably favours the low chronology, but the possibility of more than one wave of Philistine/Sea People settlement leaves some room for disagreement.

Now for some new jigsaw pieces. Monumental city walls and gates discovered in Hazor (Stratum X), Gezer (Stratum VIII) and Megiddo (Stratum Va–IVb: bear in mind that the higher stratum number represents the earlier date!), together suggesting the existence of a powerful king ruling the land, and so ascribed to Solomon on the basis of 1 Kings 9.15, which mentions Solomon as having built (or rebuilt) these three cities. The gates all had towers and six-chambers inside the entryway (three each side), set into heavy casemate walls. At Megiddo, where the stratigraphy is particularly complicated, two palaces were at first also dated to the tenth century and credited to Solomon, as were some pillared buildings identified as 'Solomon's stables'. But from his excavations at Megiddo in the 1960s and early 1970s, Yigael Yadin identified three successive strata: the Canaanite city, burned by David, the 'Solomonic' city with the walls and gates, also burned, and the later city of Ahab, which included the stables (Ahab's chariot force at the battle of Qarqar is mentioned in Shalmaneser III's Kurkh Stele).

But new sites bring new data and new calculations. Excavations at Jezreel during the 1990s uncovered a royal enclosure that, with the aid of 2 Kings 10 (it is so hard to avoid using biblical data!), was associated with Ahab, and its destruction attributed to either one of the Aramean kings in the ninth century or to Jehu's *coup*. Hence the pottery from this stratum should have correlated with the pottery from Ahab's Megiddo 'stables', but in fact it correlates with the 'Solomonic' stratum. This, unfortunately, does not settle the matter, since similar pottery was also found *under* the royal enclosure at Jezreel, so had been in use earlier. So let us interpret the evidence of destruction by fire of two strata at Megiddo: VIA, interpreted by Yadin as the last Canaanite city, burned by David, and IVA. But this city exhibits no examples of the Philistine bichrome pottery found everywhere else in the eleventh century, unlike the earlier stratum. So this city apparently dates to a later period. The Tel Aviv University excavations at Megiddo, which have been proceeding since 1984, have also concluded that the 'Solomonic' gates are later than the palaces, because the wall to which they are attached runs over the palaces. Such gates have also been found in other places and at later times and so do not necessarily point to a single builder.

And so the cause of the burning of this city must be attributed to something or someone else. The other major candidate is the Egyptian pharaoh Sheshonq, whom 1 Kings 11.40 dates to the reign of Solomon. Sheshonq left a stele in Egypt on which he claimed to have conquered 180 places in Palestine, and although he does not include Jerusalem on his list, 1 Kings 14.25 says that he did come against the city, and the traditional view therefore concludes that Sheshonq brought an end to Solomon's empire. Sheshonq also left a stele in Megiddo, but the context, and thus the dating, is not certain, and without the (dubious) biblical correlation, this campaign is hard to date exactly, but must fall within the second half of the tenth century. Sheshonq does mention Arad, however, and it has therefore been possible to correlate it with Stratum XI, now revised to Stratum XII). If Sheshonq was the destroyer of the city of the palaces, and if that city is to be dated to the same time as the Jezreel royal enclosure, this is about a century too early.

But Megiddo is a 'Finkelstein dig' and the results published support his 'low chronology'. Hazor has most recently been excavated by Mazar and Ben-Tor, and the date they give for the Iron IIA stratum X is the tenth century. Both sides are in fact now increasingly employing radiometric data, and there is a possibility, perhaps likelihood, that at some point there will be sufficient agreed data to support an agreed absolute chronology. But the calibrated dates of a single radiocarbon result may lie across the tenth and the ninth centuries BCE, so that a large number of readings is necessary. Victory for the 'low chronology' will mean the end of the United Monarchy, with the earliest stable monarchy being that of the Omrides. Some kind of short-lived local 'kingdom' under Saul has in fact recently been suggested by Finkelstein (2006a), and the significance of this may be as an alternative explanation to David of any late Iron I or IIa features in Jerusalem. Finkelstein's position should lead him to express a doubt that David ever existed, but this is an opinion that few Israeli (or American) archaeologists seem willing to voice, for reasons that may have to do with politics rather than history.

Another part of the jigsaw that is slowly becoming clearer is in the Shephelah, the lowland area between the highlands and the coastal plain, on the fringes of Philistine-controlled territory. Here too the battle between proponents of a major Jerusalem-based kingdom and those doubting it focus on the site of Tell Qeiyafa, where the excavator Yosi Garfinkel finds an Iron IIA city that for him demonstrates the existence of a Davidic kingdom. In response, others such as Nadav Na'aman suggest connecting it with the nearby city-kingdom of Gath (Na'aman 2008). Other possibilities are that such a city may have been independent or part of an as yet unknown lowland kingdom.

But the most important site of all is Jerusalem, and despite extensive excavation, had not yielded the kind of evidence that would suggest the capital of a powerful kingdom at this time. There is plenty of pottery from earlier and later periods, but not much for Iron I or IIa. Estimates of it at this time range from a small unfortified village (Jamieson-Drake 1991), to a small unfortified town with some administrative buildings (Steiner 2003), to a major capital city (Cahill in Vaughn and Killebrew 2003: 13–80). But one structure has become a focus of attention, a 'stepped stone structure', a kind of buttress at the edge of the Ophel hill, where the Iron Age city was located. This has been interpreted this as evidence of a major city, and addition, E. Mazar (2006) has uncovered a building above this structure that she thinks belongs with it and was erected by David. But archaeologists from Tel Aviv (Finkelstein 2007) have concluded that it is not a single structure and that parts of it may be Hellenistic in date! Such a discrepancy can serve as a reminder of just how open to interpretation archaeology can sometimes be.

Despite the continued manipulation of archaeology within the state of Israel (Abu el-Haj 2001) and among conservative Christian constituencies, as well as continuing disagreement and uncertainty among even responsible archaeologists, it can be said that archaeology has reached the point where it has shown itself capable of producing a coherent and accurate picture of Iron Age central Palestine. It has yet, however, to assemble the jigsaw to the point where a picture is easily recognizable, but even now that the historian will have to rely on the emerging clusters of pieces. Will this reliance mean the end of the biblical stories for the historian? Not at all; earlier chapters of this book have shown just what can be done with historical exegesis of the biblical texts, but it will be necessary to reconsider how both kinds of historical reconstruction can work together; this will be the topic of Chapter 9.

8

Sociological Approaches to History

Sociological method

Social history and sociology are not the same thing. Social history is a history of society rather than, say, of government or monarchy (politics) or warfare, and as such is merely different in focus from them. It also expresses an interest in people as groups, and in the ordinary person, as illustration the life experience of the majority of humans. Sociology will certainly embrace social history, but it also has, as a social science, a body of theory: it is a method, not a subject. To illustrate the value of a sociological approach to ancient history, we need only to consider how far, say, the biblical literature understands how people become rich, or ill, or how political power is negotiated and mediated, the use and effect of propaganda, and the impact of population growth on ecology. All these we are now very aware of as factors in our own individual and collective lives. But they play hardly any part in the biblical view of human life. Nevertheless, it is possible to try to describe the effects of these factors through analysing biblical vocabulary and reading behind the surface of the text. Such a procedure marks a strong contrast to traditional ways of reading the Bible. By contrast, sociological methods ask questions that the biblical texts neither ask nor answer. A further difference is that sociological methods cannot explain individual action except in terms of typical factors. If humans as individuals are unpredictable, as groups they are not, and while it is hard to compare individuals, this is not the case with societies.

Sociology and historiography

The approaches to modern history writing that will be discussed here are particularly congenial to combining literary and archaeological disciplines. In fact, the approaches are not altogether distinct, and might be seen as differently representing the same impulse. They all seek to distinguish, but also to combine, what we might call 'inner' and 'outer' perspectives on the past, embracing not only what people did but what they thought, including what they thought about their own past, in the belief that we cannot understand our own past without understanding human thought and perception in the past as well as human activity.

The 'Annales' approach

This is named after the journal founded by Marc Bloch and Lucien Febvre, who wished to integrate history with literature, psychology and social sciences in an attempt to recreate the totality of a society. Fernand Braudel developed such a 'total history' in his work on the Mediterranean (Braudel 1975), in which, despite its title, 'in the age of Philip II), was not, as it had been first conceived, so much about sixteenth-century Spain as about the Mediterranean itself as a place created by nature and inhabited according to the necessities of its character, illustrated by politics, trade, technology and every aspect of collective human behaviour. Structurally, the various essays that make up this book explore three different levels of historical time, or *durées*: *structure* – *longue durée* ('long time span', covering geological time and featuring geography and climate) as fundamental elements of human existence), *conjuncture* – *moyenne durée* ('medium time span', decades or centuries, economic and social time, covering major developments in social organization) and *évènement* – *courte durée* ('short time', days, weeks, months, political time, including wars). Braudel brilliantly symbolized these three as respectively ocean, tide and wave.

This is history not as a single narrative but almost as an endless soap opera in which the same setting reveals ongoing patterns of human interaction that do not generate their own momentum so much as play out the possibilities and logics of the setting. Such a narrative cannot, however, be confined to a plot or a sequence of actions or a cast of characters: the stage itself, including backstage, is part of the totality. Rather like Lévi-Strauss' structuralism, this view of the past sees human behaviour as locked into patterns of behaviour that will not be revealed by focusing on incidents but on the factors ultimately determining the limits of human choice. This is also the kind of history that archaeology is best equipped to produce, and without written sources it can hardly encroach on the *courte durée* at all.

A second important facet of *Annales* historiography is the 'history of mentalities (*mentalités*)', by which is meant the attitudes of people towards their daily life: sex, family, death, society, work – in general, 'world views'. The interest is not in merely inferring from statistics but in reconstructing the inner, psychological reality of humanity in the past. It is in effect an effort to understand culture *emically*, that is, from the inside. Among the best-known and most brilliant of such historians was Michel Foucault (e.g. 1972) who introduced a new term, *epistème*, to denote the prevailing assumptions of an era concerning knowledge and its possibility, virtually relativizing knowledge itself as a cultural product. The usefulness of a history that includes, in as scientific a way as possible, what can loosely be called the 'history of ideas' to the student of ancient Israels should be very clear, for it accords to the biblical texts, regardless of their 'historicity', a high degree of importance for understand the history of a society in which they were produced and circulated.

New Historicism

New Historicism developed in the 1980s, along with another similar, but explicitly Marxist programme known as 'cultural materialism'. The latter, originating with the work of Raymond Williams, draws on a European Marxist tradition of reflection on the interplay between economic substructure and ideological or cultural superstructure which came to recognize a mutual influence rather than the unidirectional relationship of Marx. In particular, Williams and his predecessors examined how 'hegemonic' forces in society were able to impress their views and interests on society through works of art, viewing such works under capitalist 'means of production', but were interested in how such products also betrayed signs of repressed or marginalized ('dissident') voices (Williams 1977, especially 109–14 on 'Hegemony').

New Historicism does not share either the Marxist viewpoint or the political agenda of cultural materialism. But it does seek to understand works of art (primarily literature) in a cultural context and, conversely, to reconstruct aspects of history through literature. It therefore assumes (in common with cultural materialism) that individual human actions, including artistic creation, are embedded in a network of social practice, and that literary and documentary texts are equally to come under scrutiny. However, 'new historicists' recognize that their own practices are equally subject to these principles, and cannot pretend to offer objectivity or detachment. The very process of critical analysis is also an aspect of modern capitalist culture. This is how the approach places itself between literary and social-scientific criticism. Cultural materialism also examined the way in which the reception works of art was subject to hegemonic influence, through the church or the educational system or indeed, through literary critics but without the same degree of self-reflection.

The influences on these ways of doing both literature and history together are numerous, including the anthropologist Clifford Geertz, the sociologists Karl Mannheim and Michel Foucault, the philosophers Robert Althusser and Walter Benjamin and the Frankfurt School (Adorno, Horkheimer and Habermas), none of whom can be discussed further here: the point is that we are here describing a method that has deep roots in modern European and American thought, and is not to be considered as merely one method among many, nor as one more passing fashion. (Perhaps the writer most influential on biblical scholars has been Fredric Jameson, whose *The Political Unconscious* (1981) stands somewhere between cultural materialism and New Historicism.) It should now be clear just how this kind of approach can be of enormous use to the historian of 'ancient Israel' (see Hens-Piazza 2002) and indeed, how such a use of biblical texts is already widespread in feminist and liberation theologies and ideological criticism, under the rubric of 'reading against the grain' – that is, not necessarily reading in opposition, but not simply following the direction that the text seems to be inviting, but applying one's own interests and questions.

The common procedure of a New Historicist approach is to examine the life of the author, to infer from the text the social rules that it implies, and then to determine how the historical context is reflected in the work. In doing so, the overt intentions of the author, and the priorities accorded to characters and events are ignored: minor details become particularly important just as incidental clues in a popular crime novel. In the case of the biblical literature, we do not know the author, or the time of writing, except approximately. In a good deal of previous historical work, it was common to spin a history around the dates of, for example, the various prophets, following the data usually given in the books themselves. But there now exists a suspicion that the contents, and even the individual prophets themselves, are not so easily assigned to a historical moment, that in many cases a figure from the past is being used to convey words from a quite different time. As has been explained, historical events and episodes, such as the Exodus, the wilderness wanderings, the Sinai assembly, the conquest, even perhaps the reign of David are masking some other historical context rather than revealing anything reliable about the periods they portray. How, then, is it really possible to proceed? An archaeological history, as explained in Chapter 7, is becoming ever more a realistic ambition, but no history of first millennium Palestine can simply choose to ignore the texts of the Bible, as if they played no part in that history.

'Thick description'

'Thick description' has become one of the best-known contributions to the study of culture by the anthropologist Clifford Geertz (Geertz 1973: 3–30).[1] Geertz believed that the task of anthropology is to *explain* culture rather than merely factually describe it 'thin description'). 'Thick description' includes conceptual structures and meanings, and so it entails dealing also with the interpretative functions that make up the discourse of and about any culture.

'Thick description' deals with semiotics, the science of meanings. Geertz himself states:

> Believing, with Max Weber, that man is an animal suspended in webs of significance he himself has spun, I take culture to be those webs, and the analysis of it to be therefore not an experimental science in search of law but an interpretative one in search of meaning. It is explication I am after, construing social expression on their surface enigmatical. (1973: 5)

Specifically, then, study of a culture should involve addressing the manner in which meaning is ascribed. This enables the analyst to understand how events and actions are given significance, giving access to the social discourse of that culture. In order to do this, every little detail of the culture is examined, along with its context. Ryle distinguished between a 'thin description' of, for example, a physical action, and a 'thick description' which includes the context: when and where the action took place, who performed it and their intentions in doing so. For example, the same physical act of someone 'rapidly raising and lowering their right eyelid' could be a nervous twitch, a deliberate wink to attract attention or communicate with someone, or an imitation or mockery of someone else with a nervous twitch or winking. It all depends on the context, the aims of person the performing the action, and how these were understood by others.

The term has since been adopted by new historicists of their approach to literary criticism. 'Thick description' here amounts to what is known as the 'close reading' of texts, a concept taken over and widely applied into several forms of biblical literary criticism, including the way in which the modern historian should use the biblical texts – or indeed, any ancient text, including inscriptions.

Cultural memory

It was just observed that a sociological method can give historical meaning to the making of stories about the past not as the product of an individual imagination but as the outcome of a web of individual and collective interests in the past, present and future.

To justify and explain this – and because of its intrinsic importance to the historian of ancient Israels, an understanding of collective memory, and especially collective cultural memory, a reasonably full account should be included in this *Guide*.

The problem with the use of the word 'memory' is that we customarily tend to use it of a personal recollection of something that has actually occurred in the past. All remembering is, of course, done by individuals: societies do not 'remember' in the strict sense at all. But when we replace 'memory' by 'commemory' or the established equivalent, 'commemoration', we connote a collective marking of a past event by some form of shared ritual. It has to be a ritual because, unlike personal memory, it exhibits itself only in outward demonstration. In German, however, these two are distinguished by different words: *erinnern/Erinnerung* and *gedenken/Gedächtnis* (or *andenken/Andacht*).

Personal recollection may be present in such rituals, but it is certainly not necessary. In England, the rhyme 'Remember, remember the Fifth of November' refers to the date on which a Catholic plot to blow up the Parliament in London was uncovered in 1605. It is 'remembered' by the building of bonfires, traditionally with a straw effigy of one of the conspirators, Guy Fawkes. These days increasing numbers of participants have forgotten what is 'remembered'. But in any case, the ritual probably predates 1605: it closely follows All Hallows' Eve and the lighting of the fire surely has little to do with the execution of Fawkes (he was hanged, drawn and quartered) and more with scaring away evil forces. In the USA, no one remembers the first Thanksgiving, and very few Americans can trace their descent from the first settlers in what became New England. Remembrance Day, observed in the British Commonwealth on 11 November as the date of the Armistice that ended the war of 1914–18 once remembered that war only, but the memory has now broadened to include the war of 1939–45 (or 1941–5) and, indeed, all subsequent military conflicts (America's 'Veterans' Day' falls on the same date, though a closer equivalent is Memorial Day, on the last Monday in May). These occasions do not require any personal recollection of war, or even of a specific moment, though they can provoke individual memories of lost family members or friends. In such ceremonies, then, individual memories are sometimes invoked by the ritual of a

common 'commemoration', and sometimes there are no personal
memories to be invoked at all.

Maurice Halbwachs, usually credited with formulating and
describing the notion of 'collective memory', believed than
individual memory was in fact always social, asserting that 'our
recollections depend on those of all our fellows and on the great
frameworks of the memory of society' (Halbwachs [1925] 1952:
42): even 'private' memory could only exist because of a social
context, since individuals could not reconstruct the past as a
continuum without constant social reinforcement. He proceeded
to illustrate this thesis through the various networks of memory
(family, social class, religion); he did not offer – as he frequently
did in his other sociological research – any kind of experimental
proof. As an argument he used the dream, which to him illustrated that the individual is not capable of organizing images in a
coherent way. For by 'memory', Halbwachs meant not simply an
image of the past or one embedded in a past context, but a coherent
sequence, a narrative in which each item is located relative to other
items and to a measurable distant from the present or a correlation
with a certain period of time. This is how Alan Radley (1990: 46)
puts it: 'memory is not the retrieval of stored information, but the
putting together of a claim about past states of affairs by means of
a framework of shared cultural understanding'. Such a definition
makes 'memory' very close indeed to history writing. But what
is the purpose, or the function, of such narrativizing, and such
claims about the past? Halbwachs in fact applied his method to the
creation of early Christian memory in an enterprise that has been
insufficiently followed up (though memory is now an established
component of historical Jesus studies).

Identity

However much collective and individual remembering are
cognitively and behaviourally different, they are both essential
components of identity formation. It is the narrative of memory that
carries our identity, or rather the multiple identities that we express
in different times, places and social settings. In the case of personal
memory this is dramatically illustrated in Oliver Sacks' collection
of neurological case studies *The Man Who Mistook His Wife for*

a Hat (Sacks 1986: 22–41). He describes a certain 'Lost Mariner', a man of forty-nine called 'Jimmie' who has Korsakoff's syndrome and can remember nothing of his life since the end of the Second World War including events that happened only a few minutes ago. In the late 1970s and early 1980s he still believes he is still living in 1945, the time of his latest memory. Repeatedly confronted with evidence and assertions to the contrary, he struggles to find meaning, satisfaction and happiness, constantly forgetting what he is doing from one moment to the next. Another patient has no memory at all, and has constantly to invent stories, ephemeral and contradictory, in order to sustain any kind of meaningful life. Of this man, given the name of William Thompson, Sacks writes (105):

> If we wish to know about a man, we ask 'What is his story – his real, inmost story?' – for each of us is a biography, a story. Each of us is a singular narrative, which is constructed, continuously, unconsciously, by, through, and in us – through our perceptions, our feelings, our thoughts, our actions; and, not least, our discourse, our spoken narrations. Biologically, physiologically, we are not so different from each other; historically, as narratives – we are each of us unique.

But our unique identities are constructed from social interactions with others: we define ourselves in relation to others and without different others we have no individual identity. Furthermore, as Sacks implies, our personal identities are not monolithic or static. Our identity comprises all of our social affiliations. We belong to a family, a profession, a class, maybe a gang, a political party, a supporter's club, a school. We belong with people in a neighbourhood who share familiar objects and places. Our identity can change with our role or social setting – at a football match or in a cinema or playing in an orchestra, or at a family meal, a certain strand of identity will dominate and we function collectively with others as a crowd or an audience or a team or at least in relation to them. This collective dimension of identity makes memory amenable to social analysis, which deals with groups, not individuals. In these cases the group identity interacts with the individual identity. The 'memory' that provides the script for group behaviours can be ritual, a particular kind of learned, physical memory, but can also take the form of sharing a story. Religious congregations, for example, worship by ritual but also by the commemoration of events that constitute their identity.

The most influential of recent 'mnemo-historians' (and the scholar who coined that term) is Jan Assmann who (1992: 46–9) defined 'cultural memory' as that part of collective or social memory that secures continuity of collective identity. The historian who understands that in the Bible 'Israel' is precisely this, a collective identity sustained by cultural memory, has the key to understanding the nature of biblical writing about the past.

Confabulation

Memories may be more or less reliable images of something past. But they can also distorted (they usually are), and even invented. The case of William Thompson cited above is an extreme instance of continual, even desperate confabulation, the creation of a story to cover a vacuum. Confabulation is a spontaneous account report of events that never happened, the creation of false memories, perceptions, or beliefs about the self or the environment. It is usually the result of neurological or psychological dysfunction, but it can be seen to a lesser degree in the daily behaviour of 'normal' individuals. In a famous set of experiments, Bartlett (1932) famously showed that even normal people, when asked to remember a story recently told them, confabulated. Memory fills in its own gaps: we seek a more or less complete narrative. We may have genuinely accurate images, but often make up where we need to.

The same is true of collective memories. These can confabulate and disappear, accidentally or deliberately, through collective trauma, nationalistic ideology, political correctness, dogma or simply shifts in the cultural matrix. Collectively, the Germans remember the Nazi crimes of the Second World War; the Japanese are collectively more forgetful of their own war crimes; and Turks do not openly remember the massacre of Armenians. Israel remembers the Shoah but largely submerges its own displacement of Palestinians in a 'memory' of a biblical promise to Abraham. In retaliation, the Palestinians tend to 'forget' the Shoah and deny the existence of an 'ancient Israel' at all. Nearly every violent conflict on earth arises out remembered narrative, or is justified by it, since the past, where identity has to be born, and the present, where it resides, have to be reconciled, whether by truth or confabulation or a mixture of the two. For the historian dealing with biblical narratives, confabulation defines the creation of events and characters that never occurred or existed. The words 'fraud', 'lie' or 'forgery' betray a very unsophisticated understanding of how memory works: we should rather accept that inventiveness of all sorts is an inevitable aspect of collective remembering that reveals something of the nature of the society that is 'remembering'.

Memory need not be confined to time, but can also involve space. In human geography, notions of real objectively measured space sometimes given way to the analysis of perceived or socially produced space (Lefebvre 1991; Soja 1971): we get (on Lefebvre's analysis) the 'perceived [first] space' of everyday social life, the 'conceived [second] space' of maps or urban plans or architects, and a 'lived [third] space' created by art (extremely represented in cubism and surrealism). The *Mappa Mundi* in Hereford Cathedral bears a thirteenth-century depiction of the world, which depicts imagined space and imagined time together, with illustrations of human history, such as the fate of Lot's wife, embedded. Here is a biblically derived 'lived space'. So, in the biblical narratives, is 'Canaan' and 'Israel's land', and so in many Bible atlases we have a mixture of second and third kinds of spaces. The Bible places Jerusalem at the centre of Israel's life and imagination; Palestine is transformed into the 'Holy Land'. Yet while space is something in which we are all constantly located, the past is not directly accessible. We can measure it calendrically ('second time') but as history, that is to say as a narrative bearing meaning, it belongs to third time as well. The modern historian can observe and measure both the 'lived spaces' and the 'lived times' of the ancient writers in creating their past.

Does 'cultural memory' differ from 'tradition'? Biblical scholars, aware of a certain tension between fact and biblical story, yet caught in the requirements of an apparently 'historical' religion, adopted the word 'tradition' (this is particularly true of German scholars, for whom *Überlieferung and Tradition* overlap) to imply a kind of link between event and record and also, one suspects, to endow the story with some kind of authority. Nevertheless, a famous collection of essays under the title *The Invention of*

Tradition (Hobsbawm and Ranger 1984) did much to establish the modern suspicion of 'tradition' as embodying a bogus claim. Many cherished British traditions were shown to be of fairly recent origin and with little or no historical veracity. 'Tradition' remains a perfectly respectable term for the maintenance of social identity through inherited narratives, but 'cultural memory', as an aspect of collective memory has the advantage of a body of data and theory rooted in neuroscience, psychology and sociology. It also redirects the focus of the researcher to the act of remembering and its function rather than the extent of historicity behind the content. This is important, because in this way it redirects away from an invented history towards a real history, a history of remembering.

Assmann, as mentioned earlier, coined the term 'mnemo-history' to designate the 'history of the memory of the past', the study of how and what people remembered in the past about the past. But of course that study includes how we remember today too, which is where the mnemo-history of the Bible is fascinating, because while biblical stories represent cultural memories of (mostly) Judeans some 2,000–2,500 years ago, they also continue to function as contemporary cultural memories for Jews and Christians for whom the biblical story is also part of an identity. Archaeology too is a vehicle of cultural memory, through which, for example, the State of Israel is, through all kinds of media, creating an 'ancient Israelite space' that while engaging with past reality, has just as much to do with memory (Shavit 1997; Abu el-Haj 2001; Kletter 2005). Yet all modern histories, despite being subject to rules of evidence and argument, can be understood as to some extent vehicles of cultural memory. It is unavoidable. Yet good histories can also correct and dispel cultural memories that claim to represent a factual past yet do not. If an absolute accurate memory is impossible to achieve, it is still possible, and desirable, to expose a false one if it attracts belief as a true account. Yet memories and critical histories can coexist even where they contradict one another so long as their different functions and values are understood and accepted. Many Jews believe that the Exodus did not happen, many Christians accept that the story of Jesus's birth is highly legendary. But this doubt does not necessarily devalue the story, nor dismantle the identity that the story affirms. There is a striking body of critical historical scholarship dealing with Jewish (and Christian) collective memory, both ancient (e.g. Halbwachs 1952; Mendels 2004,

2007) and modern (Yerushalmi 1982; Zerubavel 2003; Zerubavel 2005; Mendels 2007): that is, whether or not these authors would consent to the name, 'mnemo-history'.

Cold and hot histories

We conclude this chapter with Lévi-Strauss's distinction between 'hot' and 'cold' societies (see Lévi-Strauss 1962: 217–44: 'Time Regained'). According to this analysis, modern cultures that remained open to diverging influences were 'hot', while those that change little over time were 'cold'. The former are dynamic and even entropic, while the latter maintain order, conserving their original state as far as possible, and thus appear not to progress or evolve. Therefore they reject (or rather, perhaps, do not understand) the notion of 'history'.

Assmann develops this notion in his work on cultural memory. He stresses that not every society is necessarily either a 'hot' or a 'cold' one; within a single culture there will be elements of both forms of remembering (1992: 69–70). The use of writing, which Lévi-Strauss had identified as characterizing 'hot' societies because it freezes a record of the past so that later readers can see for themselves the extent to which their present differs, does not, in Assmann's view, necessarily achieve that result, arguing that in Egypt, writing did not at first create a sense of history at all. More important, in his view, are traumatic events that radically change ways of living, necessitating a confrontation with the fact of historical change. In Egypt, it was foreign domination by Persians and Macedonians that produced histories, while in Judah, it was the deportation to Babylonia, and in Greece the experiences of war with Persia, as well as the creation of new forms of political life, that led the emergence of historical enquiry. In the creation of canons, Assmann (1992: 103–29) sees a mechanism for holding together both 'cold' and 'hot' elements of memory, that is, of harnessing both stabilizing and dynamic forces. But, while it may seem that myths serve cold memories of the past and histories hot ones, this is not necessarily true, because some myths may highlight the gap between an idealized state of affairs and the present one, inviting members of the society to strive for the ideal.

In his discussion of religion as memory, Assmann deals in detail with Deuteronomy and its recollection of the Exodus events (see also the treatment of Deuteronomy in the next chapter). Rogerson (2010: 25–41) has taken up this theme, exploring the contrast between the 'Deuteronomistic' history (Joshua–Kings) and the books of Chronicles as respectively 'hot' and 'cold'. It was explained in Chapters 4 and 6 that Chronicles presents a definition of 'Israel' as unchanging and the temple as persisting from the time of David onwards as the eternal core of religious life. Rogerson cites several other examples of the way in which these writers in many episodes promote a sense of order and minimize historical disruption, as compared with the parallel accounts in Kings, where Israel's (or Judah's) fortunes are always changing in the light of royal religious (or political) policy. Chronicles, says Rogerson, stresses continuity, Kings disruption; and so the former leaves little scope for a desire or expectation of change in the future, while Kings leaves the future very uncertain, and the difference between them is to some extent explained (in line with Assmann's understanding) as due to the different historical contexts of the authors.

For Rogerson the context of the Deuteronomistic History is the aftermath of the fall of Samaria and the depradations of Sennacherib, but it works equally well if a later context, after the conversion of Judah to a poor and quite neglected province with a small and insignificant capital city. Whether the context of Chronicles (probably somewhere around 350–300 BCE) was in fact as untroubled as its 'cold' history implies we simply do not know from lack of sources. But we might also conclude that both 'hot' and 'cold' histories might be generated in order to counter a prevailing mood: to assure continuity in a time of frightening change, or express a belief in change when the situation seemed depressingly static. It is possible to see the difference between the two types of utilizing (or creating) the past without accepting a determinate explanation. Cultural memory can be manipulated by the ruling elite and its literate retainers and does not have simply to reflect a social consensus. This does not mean, however, that the act of literary remembering has no relationship with its historical context, for clearly it does. In any event, Rogerson's extensive examples illuminate very clearly the differences in temperature between the biblical historiographies and the extent to which their varying portraits are explicable less by determining matters of historical accuracy and more by the function of the story as a demonstration of what history is about.

The study of cultural memory has become a major component of the study of religion in general, as part of a growing engagement with a cognitive science approach to question of human religious belief. This takes us well beyond the scope of this book, but such developments show the increasing reach of social science paradigms, sometimes with the aid of the natural sciences, into the study of religion, theology and philosophy – as well as history. Much more could be said of other aspects of sociological theory that might be usefully applied by the historian of 'ancient Israels'. But the point has perhaps been made fully enough.

Sociology in biblical studies

The use of sociology in studies of Israel and Judaism goes back to Max Weber, but little or no use was made of his insights in twentieth-century history writing about ancient Israels. To consider sociology as an explicit component of modern history writing we can go back to Gottwald's 1979 *The Tribes of Yahweh: A Sociology of the Religion of Liberated Israel 1250–1050 B.C.E.* At the opening of his book (5–7), he writes of the 'scandal of sociological method', following with a chapter on 'Complementarity of Humanistic and Sociological Studies of Early Israel' (8–17).

What Gottwald means by 'sociological method' is an approach that eschews theological categories which bypass the usual categories of historical explanation, that synthesizes different insights and perspectives and renders an account of the totally social reality, of its 'total existence as a social system' (7). In particular, Gottwald criticized the class orientation of the typical biblical that engendered a certain sympathy towards monarchic, aristocratic and then bourgeois interests (11). Gottwald's approach is indebted to both Marx and to Weber, each stressing the connection between economics and religion, Marx the role of class and Weber the need for *Verstehen*, an understanding of both the intention and the context of human action. Gottwald's proposal was that the radical character of Israel's religion was shaped by a certain social-economic egalitarian system. Gottwald was able to create this thesis because, following the West Bank Survey, he located early Israel within the economic and political context of Canaan, regarding it as a reaction, a revolt, against the structures of the city-states. The biblical materials, of which Joshua and Judges form the primary resource, are then analysed for clues to the actual social structures, which include people, tribe, protective association (*mišpaḥah*), house and father's house, the twelve-tribe system as a whole. A further section contrasts sociology of religion and biblical theology and elaborates the religion of this new society from three directions: idealist, structural-functional (the regnant social-anthropological model) and cultural-materialist (the archaeological model; the last two are not mutually exclusive).

The main flaws in Gottwald's great work are his early dating of the religion that he described, which now seems to have begun to crystallize only in the post-monarchic era, and an over-positive use of the sources for historical reconstruction. One might also detect a very American bias towards egalitarianism and against monarchy (though the Marxist-materialist approach is quite un-American). But the book achieved an important breakthrough in formulating the question of Israelite origins and religion as a social revolution not a divine revelation or the achievements of a great individual. It certainly made a contribution to liberation theology in attending to issues of poverty and subsistence and economic exploitation, and it led directly to a major collaborative project (in which Gottwald participated) called the sociology of the monarchy, which advanced from the era of social formation to its transformation into monarchy, using sociological models of the origins of states. From this issued a series of monographs entitled 'The Social World of Biblical Antiquity' (for a list of volumes in this series, see Chapter 10). This Society of Biblical Literature venture in turn spun off another, on the sociology of the Second Temple, which was inspired not only because it seemed logical to take the historical periodization a step on, but also from the belief of some of its protagonists that this was the period when the biblical texts could properly be studied sociologically, this being their time of production. From that likewise four volumes of a 'Sociology of the Second Temple' series were derived (details also in Chapter 10).

Since then, sociological models have been applied, for example, to the political systems of empires (using Eisenstadt 1963), as a way of explaining the experiences of Samaria and Judah as imperial provinces. These measures include deportation (Oded 1979), and several fairly recent studies have focused on the mechanism of adaptation to exile – or rather, as it is coming to be called, deportation or even 'forced migration' (Ahn 2010). The sociological aspect of this study is found particularly in its relation to migration in other times and places, thus including comparative analysis. Surprisingly, the Qumran manuscripts initially drew very little sociological analysis, even when recognized as probably sectarian (Talmon [1988] being an honourable exception); more recently this has been rectified (e.g. Regev 2007; Baumgarten 1997; Blenkinsopp 2006; Chalcraft [ed.] 2008).

Among other scholars illustrating the value of a sociological approach is N. P. Lemche, who dismantled (1976) the amphictyony model of Noth. But even more importantly he illustrated a central feature of ancient (and much modern) social systems, namely patronage (1995). Patronage supplies a very eloquent illustration of the contrast of theological and socio-economic vocabulary. A central concept of much Old Testament theology has been 'covenant', and in the second part of the twentieth century the political root of the conception was exposed, in the form of treaties between client and patron monarchs, especially Hittite and Assyrian. The patron king imposing obligations on a vassal client seems to have been the model for a theory of religion in which a people became vassals in return for a divine king's protection. The theologically important but hard-to-translate Hebrew word ḥesed, often translated as 'lovingkindness' or 'grace', which is applied to both the deity and his subjects can now be understood not primarily as a religious or theological concept but one that denotes the obligations of both patron and client: protection on the one hand and on the other 'respect' (those having seen *The Godfather* will recognize such reciprocity immediately).

Sociological approaches and perspectives are still not routinely deployed in the writing of histories of 'ancient Israel', but they are indispensable in understanding many aspects of the biblical sources and relating them to social reality: how narratives about the past are generated and why they take the form they do, the mechanisms of forming literary canons (Davies 1998 for an explicitly cultural approach to the question), the ideological influence of the state and the power of the scribal class in mediating it but also critiquing it. Of course, as especially religious critics will say, a sociological analysis is not objectively better than a religious one as historical explanation, for it entails its own materialist, secular presuppositions. This is true, but even more important is the fact that theological or religious explanations cannot generate history in the sense of describing and explaining human action. The sociological method allows us to write a history of Israels that can be understood as part of the totality of ancient human history and indeed it welcomes this kind of historian into the ranks of historians generally.

PART FOUR

Constructing a History of 'Ancient Israel'

9

Synthesizing Data and Approaches

The foregoing chapters have made the case that literary and archaeological and sociological narratives of the past – if we can simply
a bit – have each a different character, ask different questions and
produce different kinds of stories about the past. It may indeed be
ideal to keep these kinds of narrative apart, but the historian of
Israel does not really have the choice of abandoning either Bible
or archaeology. In the next chapter a few examples will be given
of how recent historians have undertaken their task. Here we shall
focus on three issues that illustrate different problems of combining
evidence and choosing the right data.

'Minimalism'

This also seems a convenient place to speak about 'minimalism'
because the term, with its opposite, 'maximalism' have come to
designate, rather lazily, two alternative approaches to the practice
of writing a history of ancient Israels. 'Minimalist' is a term
used to characterize what was has been seen by more traditional
scholars as an overly sceptical and even nihilistic approach to the
biblical narratives. In fact, the real issue is not how much biblical
'historicity' remains after the historian has done the work, because
'historicity' is, or should not be, the guiding principle or aim of
any historian. The issue is much deeper, and rests ultimately on

what history is, how we know history and the role of ideology in the production of history, by writers in both the ancient and modern world. On this criterion, 'minimalism' is not to be seen as the ideologically driven programme of a small group, but the application of an approach that has been adopted, in whole or in part, by a fairly large number of scholars in response to the collapse of 'biblical archaeology' and the absolute necessity of reconsidering the way in which archaeological data and biblical texts are best related in the search for a critical history.

'Minimalist' logic argues that once it has been established that biblical narratives about Israelite origins are of dubious historical value, the historian can hardly adopt the premise that biblical stories be taken as historical unless or until proven otherwise. If the stories of the Pentateuch, of Joshua and possibly also of Judges, are not capable of serving as a template for a modern history, it seems right to question any narrative bereft of supporting evidence – and thus must include the figures of David and Solomon as much as Abraham, Joseph or Moses. David seems, in fact, to be a more crucial figure than the others mentioned, perhaps because he is symbolic of the presence and the achievements of 'Israel' in Palestine, a secular rather than a religious icon. Hence, 'minimalism' has often been popularly portrayed as denying the existence of this figure, while Abraham, Moses and Joshua have, with relatively little protest, been allowed to lapse from history into legend. The dispute over David is a political rather than a historical issue, because Judaism is now embodied in a political state.

But as far as historical method is concerned, 'minimalism' represents a return in several ways to the position achieved by Wellhausen in the late nineteenth century. Reinhard Kratz (2012) makes the observation that Wellhausen's distinction between the religion of 'ancient Israel' and the religion of Judaism remains a fundamentally important insight, and while we can, of course, now entertain a much richer, complex and more positive appreciation of early Judaism or Judaisms, and archaeology has allowed us to discover a rather different view of the religious practices in Iron Age Israel and Judah than Wellhausen conceived, the notion that Judaism invented the biblical Israel, and not the other way round, if it can be put so bluntly, follows the insight of Wellhausen, or, even earlier, of de Wette. It would be perfectly reasonable to describe both these scholars as 'minimalist' both in their method and their conclusions.

The principle properly described by the label 'minimalist' is that biblical texts betray the history of the period of their production, and it has been followed in this *Guide*. The principle does not in itself rule out the historicity of any particular biblical event or figure at all, but it does insist that unless we have evidence other than a biblical story, we cannot accept any claim for historicity, because in themselves, the narratives do not prove anything about their content; what they do constitute is evidence of themselves, as stories once told, and the historian's first question is: why was this story told, and what does this story tell us about its writers and hearers or readers?

A new 'biblical archaeology'?

In the decades of dispute and negotiation between the biblical text and archaeology several different methodologies have been proposed. The procedure of twentieth-century 'Biblical archaeology' was to seek events and circumstances in the archaeological record that 'confirm' or 'correspond to' or 'converge with' elements of the biblical story, picking up one example after another, like pottery sherds in a survey. Because most archaeologists working on Iron Age Palestine are knowledgeable about the biblical story, this is an easy and attractive option. Here is an example from a recent book on archaeological data about 'ancient Israel': '[i]n contrast to previous studies, archaeological evidence constitutes the main source of information for this work, while the information that can be obtained from the Bible ... will be presented, in most cases, as an additional and complementary tool' (Faust 2012a: 2). The 'information obtained from the Bible', however, is not necessarily historical information at all: it has not been critically processed, but read straight from the page, in classical 'biblical archaeology' style. No doubt this manner of fitting scraps of biblical narrative into an archaeological history will continue.

Nevertheless, as the quote also shows, and as explained in Chapter 7, the view is gaining ground that the history of ancient Israel and Judah can be left to archaeology alone. The belief that in the end the spade can have the verdict, without putting the Bible anywhere, is an initially attractive one, but just how independent of the biblical stories *is* the archaeology in the first place? How much does it rely on biblical place names, and even on figures whose existence is otherwise unknown (not just David and Solomon, but the majority of Israelite and Judahite monarchs)?

The opposite view, that history can remain as a kind of rationalizing paraphrase of the biblical story is hardly to be encountered these days, though a lot of biblical scholarship still operates in something of a historical vacuum, projecting historical contexts without regard to archaeology, anthropology or sociology. On the whole, however, biblical scholars are aware of the inadequacy of that very term, recognizing the necessity of integrating exegesis with archaeological data. But perhaps not sufficiently recognized is just how partial the archaeological data often are, and just how provisional, open to dispute and subject to ideological bias archaeological interpretation can be. It is not helpful to insist that overall either biblical texts or archaeological data should predominate in the production of a history. Rather, the question is how the stories that each kind of data can tell can and should be combined in appropriate ways. As explained in Chapter 7, archaeology is increasingly inferring the functioning of households, distribution of gender roles, belief systems, symbolic universes, ethnicity, and many other issues that will illuminate the social setting of biblical narratives. Conversely, literary-critical exegesis can amplify, explain and perhaps adjudicate on incomplete or contested archaeological data. The essential principle for the utilization of both kinds of evidence is that both literary-historical exegesis and archaeology are human sciences. Biblical scholarship is no longer a theological science (whatever that may mean), and the biblical texts may no longer be presented by the scholar as disclosing the nature and activity of a god. But they are telling us about how human beings, individually and collectively, imagined and lived as if gods existed, how the thoughts and behaviours of people were informed and controlled by those who claimed to have access to the gods, and who had the power to declare, or even decree, what had happened, what was happening and what would happen in the future. History is a branch of the study of humans, and in this enterprise the interpretation of texts and of material remains are in principle collaborative.

If this point needs to be made more concrete, let us not forget that literary-historical criticism entails the hypothesis of an artefact. In the case of literary-historical exegesis, this has a rather acute sense. In reconstructing the history of a text, we are in effect hypothesizing or reconstruction an artefact, one that we date to a particular time, place and kind of author. The artefact was not, of course, recovered by the spade, but in theory, if it existed, it might have been, as the Qumran biblical manuscripts were. In that case, we have a fairly precise historical context, but not the context of the earlier versions of the manuscripts. These have to be inferred from the contents. Nevertheless, the idea of a 'reconstructed literary artefact' is entailed in most historical-critical exegesis and as such it is intervening in the realm of archaeology, too. *How* biblical stories of the past, archaeological data and sociological analysis should be utilized in any given case will not often be agreed, but it is undeniable that they *must* all be brought into play as casting light on human life in a particular episode in our human past.

Case studies

What follow are three important case studies which are meant to illustrate shortcomings, challenges and opportunities.

Jerusalem and text production

The contribution of archaeology to our understanding of sixth- and fifth-century BCE Judah has opened up several important questions. Biblical stories of wholesale deportation and empty land, of dramatic restoration but of almost complete silence about seventy years or more of Judahite history, can now be assessed from the results of surveys and excavations. Who lived in Judah after 586, and where? How poor was the economy? How did it recover, if at all? Other questions, such as when Jerusalem and its temple were rebuilt are not so easily solved, nor why Jerusalem was re-established as the capital and chief sanctuary of the province. This is the time and place are where many biblical scholars place the composition of a good deal of the biblical texts – including those thought to have been composed or edited in 'exile' and brought back to Judah. In a few recent articles, however, Israel Finkelstein (e.g. 2008, 2009) has advanced an argument based purely on archaeology, deducing from the rubble from a small excavation (not by him) on the Temple mount, and from remains on the Ophel hill – the 'so-called 'City of David', the Iron Age location of the city, south of the Temple Mount – that Jerusalem in the Persian and Early Hellenistic periods at this time had a very small population. He concludes that the northern part of the ridge of the 'City of David' was uninhabited, the southern part of the ridge was probably uninhabited as well, and the population was confined to the central part of the ridge, a total of 20–5 dunams, according to his estimate containing 400–500 people, of whom there were 100 adult men. He concludes: 'On a broader issue, the archaeological evidence from Jerusalem casts severe doubt on the notion that much of the biblical material was composed in the Persian and Early Hellenistic periods' (2008: 514).

In a private exchange, I asked Finkelstein when and where he thought Haggai, Zechariah, Second Isaiah, Chronicles, and ben Sira were written, and he replied that this was not his problem. I replied that these writing were artefacts and it was his job as much as mine, if he claimed to be doing history and not just archaeology, to explain them. It is only fair to point out that Finkelstein, more than any Israeli archaeologist, does try to engage with biblical scholarship (see next chapter), and has co-written two articles with the biblical scholar Thomas Römer on the figures of Abraham and Jacob (2014a, 2014b). But here is a very clear case of biblical texts as artefacts that provide historical knowledge: the knowledge that in Jerusalem at this time, literary texts were being written and edited.

In any case, it is important to remember that archaeological reasoning can also be challenged. Finkelstein's analysis is imperfect on several counts. He has not been able to accurately estimate settlement on the Temple mount, where in fact the bulk of the population may have lived, since Jerusalem was a temple and palace city. For the same reason, a disproportionate number of the population may have been priests and scribes, whose families did not necessarily live in the city. How many men does it take to write a book and maintain an archive and a library (both institutions obviously necessary for provincial administration and for a central temple)? But the question can go further: if the production of biblical books, including authoring and editing and copying, was undertaken by a small elite numbering tens, sufficient to service temple and palace and no more, that information helps to clarify other very important issues such as the number of copies of a text that may have existed at any one time, to explain the conservatism of Hebrew language and style in the scriptural corpus, to assess the degree of knowledge among all the scribes of that corpus, and the likely extent to which the contents of the corpus were known outside a small circle. The sociology of text production is precisely an area in which biblical exegesis and archaeology need to collaborate. Archaeologists and exegetes need to query each other's data, for here we have a problem that needs sharing and cooperatively investigating.

Israel and Judah as separate 'houses'

Evidence from excavation and surveys in the West Bank survey, which has continued to be analysed, and with increasing clarity, shows a difference not only in the onset of Iron I settlement, but subsequently in the rate of political and social development and in social habits, between the populations of the northern and southern central highlands of Palestine, suggesting that they originated independently and remained separated for some time. There is no hint from the archaeological data to justify regarding the two populations as comprising a single society or subsequently a single state: that is, no archaeological evidence of an 'ancient Israel'. The question was discussed in one chapter of Thompson's 1992 *Early History of the Israelite People*; but only archaeological evidence was addressed, even though there was a section on the 'Intellectual Matrix of Biblical Tradition'. But historical-critical exegesis can contribute much to this question. As reviewed earlier, the Pentateuch unambiguously describes a twelve-tribe 'Israel' without any indication of a separate Judah, and yet the books of Samuel speak of two 'houses' of Israel and Judah which develop into the two 'kingdoms' of Judah and Israel in the books of Kings. There is no narrative explanation of how Judah became a separate 'house', nor of how and why it formed its own kingdom. The 'house of Judah' emerges first in the text at 1 Samuel 17, where in the battle against the Philistines, 'men of Judah' suddenly materialize among 'men of Israel'. The transition from twelve tribes to eleven-plus-one, however, is not quite unanticipated: in Joshua and Judges, Judah is already acquiring some kind of special status, though still as a member of a single twelve-tribe entity. For example, only Judah successfully conquers all its allotted land; and Judah provides the first of the judges. There is also a premonition of the conflict between Judahite David and Benjaminite Saul in Judges 17–21, with clear links to the figure of Saul, via the towns of Gibeah and Jabesh-Gilead.

The books of Samuel and Kings, in other words, portray Israel and Judah as distinct entities already from the time of Saul: or, in other words, the twelve-tribe Israel of Genesis to Judges is now an eleven-tribe 'house'. Perhaps this portrayal is the outcome of a wish on the part of Judahite historiographers to distance Judah from Israel: but if so, why the story of the United Monarchy as an ideal? Can we maintain the plausibility of a twelve-tribe society, or is the portrait of Samuel–Kings more reliable? The latter, in fact, is fits the archaeology better, and from this, other questions arise. How does the historian unravel the apparently tight relationship between the characters of Samuel, Saul and David (for a radical suggestion, see Auld 2011). What historical context gives rise to a story of a struggle between Judah and Benjamin and their royal champions within a wider conflict between the houses of Judah and Israel? The collocation of these two disputes together may well suggest a fifth- or early fourth-century Jerusalem setting when the transfer of power from Jerusalem to Benjaminite territory and/or vice versa may have involved friction between rival elites (such a possibility was raised by Edelman 2001), while relations with Samaria seem to have become a matter of disagreement within Judah itself, as the range of literature from this period attests.

Here, then, there are different dimensions of a single issue in which either archaeology or exegesis is interested and is able to tackle, but also in which there is actually a basic agreement: that the original separate emergence of Israel and Judah is indicated both settlement data and by the books of Samuel and Kings.

The Exodus

For centuries, the reciting of the Exodus story has been the central ritual of Jewish identification, one shared by religious and non-religious Jews. For much of the twentieth century attempts were made to verify such an event, but archaeologically it is impossible to do so, and what we know of Egyptian power in the Late Bronze Age make any such event (even stripped of the miraculous and legendary features) very unlikely. The picture of early Iron Age populations provided from surveys and excavations does not leave room for the influx of a large foreign population. But how did this story arise, if not from some such event? Is it a disguised rehearsal of escape from Egyptian hegemony in Palestine by a group that later found itself among the agriculturalists of the central hills? Is it an amalgam of numerous flights from Egypt by Palestinian residents who had once fled there in times of famine? Is it a confabulation? Of all the questions likely to be asked of a historian of 'ancient Israel', the Exodus, perhaps with the figure of David, is likely to be the most pressing – and both are difficult to explain simply.

The great foundation legend of Exodus, Sinai and wilderness wandering that form the bulk of the Pentateuch cannot be fruitfully investigated by starting with the search for a possible historical core. It can be affirmed that migration from Palestine to Egypt, and presumably back again, is a common pattern of Palestine's *longue durée*, necessitated by Egypt's security and fertility and the occasional famine in Palestine. Indeed, Genesis 12 has a tale of Abraham doing just that, and the family of Jacob does likewise in Genesis 42. Possibly, the story is an amalgam of such experiences. But that hardly explains why the story has been meshed into the account of the origins of Israel itself. A more fruitful approach may be to work backwards. If we take the view that the Pentateuchal text as it has been preserved goes back at least to the fourth century, we can address two major lines of investigation, for at the end of the fourth century we have not only the 'Israelite' version, but two Egyptian versions; moreover, these Egyptian versions are also in a secondary sense, Judahite/ Judean, because they present the story as being about the origins of Judeans/Jews, not 'Israelites' (the word 'Israel' is never used, and Samaria is ignored).

The fullest Egyptian 'Exodus' story is cited by the first-century CE Jewish historian Josephus Flavius (*Against Apion* I.73–105) who quotes from Manetho, the early third-century Greco-Egyptian historian, about an ancient invasion of Egypt by a people called 'Hyksos' (understood to mean 'shepherds' in Egyptian), who occupied Egypt for 511 years and who were finally driven back and confined to an area called Avaris which they fortified. Unsuccessful in capturing this stronghold, the Egyptian king Thummosis came to an agreement with them by means of which they left; and 240,000 consequently left and travelled to Syria. They built a city 'in that country that is now called Judea ... and called it Jerusalem'. (Remember that Jerusalem is nowhere mentioned in the Pentateuch.)

A second excerpt from Manetho (*Apion* I.228–52) concerns a king Amenophis who, centuries after the 'shepherds' had been driven out by 'Tethmosis', wished to rid his country of lepers and other diseased persons, 80,000 of whom were sent east of the Nile to work in quarries. Some leprous priests were sent to the old Hyksos capital of Avaris, and these appointed a ruler among them called Osarsiph, a priest of Heliopolis, who made them forswear the Egyptian gods and follow new laws. Osarsiph then wrote to the 'shepherds' in Jerusalem and invited them to assist him in a war against Amenophis. Subsequently the Jerusalemites did invade Egypt and behaved cruelly. Osarsiph, once he had joined the Jerusalemites, came to be known as Moses. Amenophis, having returned from Ethiopia, then drove the shepherds and the lepers back to Syria.

Accepting (correctly) that Manetho was consulting ancient Egyptian records, Josephus accepts that he is accurately conveying ancient sources, saying that 'these shepherds ... were none other than our ancestors'; but he rejects the second story, arguing that Manetho has abandoned his ancient chronicles and produced 'rumour' and 'incredible stories'.

We find elements of Manetho's story in a near-contemporary Greek writer who visited Egypt, Hecataeus of Abdera, whose writings have, again, only been preserved by others, here Diodorus of Sicily (40.3); a further excerpt from his book 'written entirely about the Jews', is also cited in Josephus, but its authenticity remains disputed. Hecataeus knows of only one story of Judeans leaving Egypt. A pestilence in Egypt at some time (Hecataeus

gives no chronological clues) prompted the inhabitants to expel
certain strangers who practised alien rites; of these deportees, some
landed in Greece, but the larger number in Judea, which was then
uninhabited. They settled under the leadership of Moses, who
founded several cities, including Jerusalem, where he established
a temple. He also set up 'forms of worship and ritual', laws and
political institutions. He divided the people into twelve tribes,
forbade images to be made of their sole deity, and appointed
priests, who were to be not only in charge of the cult but also
political leaders and judges. (Thus, he says, 'the Jews have never
had a king' but are ruled by a high priest, who enjoys great power
and prestige.) Moses, continues the account, also instituted a
military education and led the people to many conquests against
neighbouring tribes, after which he apportioned the land equally,
but reserving larger portions for the priests. The sale of land was
forbidden, specifically so as to avoid oppression of the poor by
the rich through accumulation of land. The Judeans' laws claim to
have been words heard by Moses from God.

Hecataeus seems to have derived some of this information
from Judean sources, but there are of course discrepancies. He
may also have known the same story as Manetho, but his own
version is not anti-Judean. It remains just possible that the narratives of Hecataeus and Manetho are a garbled form of a Judean
story of an 'exodus', in which the plagues, the name of Moses
and the departure of a group of people to(wards) Judah have
been transformed. The nature of contacts between Judeans and
Egyptians between 600 and 300 BCE makes it very likely that the
story developed through interaction. At the capture of Jerusalem by
Nebuchadrezzar in 586 BCE (2 Kgs 25.26 may contain some truth)
many Judeans went to Egypt. Jeremiah 43–4 expresses hatred both
of these Judean immigrants and of Egypt, threatening destruction
at the hand of the Babylonians, and in 44.1 and 15 the locations
of Judean communities are named as Migdol, Tahpanes, Memphis
and Pathros (Pathros denotes Upper Egypt, where Elephantine–
Syene lay). According to *Aristeas* 12–14 Ptolemy III (246–221)
later transported thousands of Judeans to Egypt as military
colonists and slaves. In the early second century BCE a high priest
from Jerusalem, Onias IV, fled with his supporters to Leontopolis
and built a temple there. The large Jewish population of Alexandria
was one of the consequences of this history of Judean immigration

to Egypt, and the conflicts between Jews and Egyptians in this city are well documented.

There is, accordingly, an almost continuous process of Judahite/ Judean settlement in Egypt over the entire Iron Age (as no doubt before as well). A degree of knowledge among Egyptians and immigrant Judahites/Judeans of each other's stories is to be expected, and especially a story celebrated annually by all Judeans; and among such stories may have been one about the origin of the Judean race in Egypt. The historian might consider a milieu in which Judeans in Egypt, reflecting an ambivalent attitude towards the host culture, tell a story about defeating the pharaoh. But in doing so, did they transform an anti-Semite or even anti-Judean Egyptian story, revived in opposition to another wave of immigrants, turning imported disease into miraculous plagues and expulsion into escape? This explanation encounters the difficulty of assigning some kind of Exodus story to no earlier than the fifth-century Judah, however, and of explaining how it became a foundation story for both Judahites and Samarians.

So perhaps we can go back a little further and also invoke the topics of identity and cultural memory. It seems that the Exodus story functioned as a mechanism by which at least one 'ancient Israel' was created. It may not have been the only origin story preserved in the scriptures, for the stories of the ancestors Abraham, Isaac and Jacob and of the conquest of the land under Joshua also may have fulfilled that role. But the canonical story of Exodus and lawgiving formed the spine of the annual festival cycle of Jerusalem (and also Gerizim) and thus came to constitute the definitive memory of how Israel began through divine election and how it acquired its distinctive constitution (its Torah, its *mišpatim*) by divine revelation.

To trace this history of the creation of 'Israel', and the place of the Exodus story in it, a useful starting point may be the story in 2 Kings 17 (already discussed in Chapter 6) which describes a deliberate process of enculturation, and while its historicity is a matter of debate, coheres well with what can be inferred from Deuteronomy. The question of imperial authorization in this story is perhaps also significant, since although it seems unlikely in the case of Assyria there has been a lot of discussion recently about the creation of the Mosaic Torah as the result of Persian imperial authorization (see conveniently Watts 2001). The 'Israel' created through memory of Exodus and lawgiving is on this perspective not a product of two neighbouring kingdoms but two fraternal provinces, after a period of crisis, when former tribal, political and religious identities were disrupted.

Whether such a process of 'Israelite' nation-building as reflected in Deuteronomy actually took place s an organized programme, and if so, if it originated in Samaria or Judah remains to be established. The story of Josiah's law book, which is quite probably an effort to not only endow Deuteronomy with a monarchic authorization, underscoring its continuity with the former identity, but also to Judaize it, might lead one to suspect that the contents of Deuteronomy originated in Israel/Samaria. But why the story of an escape from Egypt would function as the occasions for the national foundation myth of an Israelite 'people' remains unclear; equally unclear is whether we can trace such a story beyond the seventh century BCE at the earliest.

An investigation into the Exodus story is one that does not depend on, let alone give priority, to archaeological research. Like the figures of Moses and the Torah, it belongs at the beginning of the monotheistic and aniconic cult of Judah and Samaria, whose worshippers constitute an *ethnos* of twelve tribes: the very 'people of Israel'.

Postscript

It has been made clear that a competent historian of 'ancient Israel(s)' needs to be able to handle a wide range of disciplines, but especially those of the literary-historical critic and the archaeologist. How is such expertise acquired? Archaeologists and biblical scholars have separate formations, recognize largely separate goals, and are institutionally and professionally isolated. By contrast, many biblical scholars, if they can find the time, participate in digs where, although they do not contribute much of their professional expertise, they learn archaeological practice. There are also conferences and conversation that bring the two kinds of expertise together. But how many exegetes can have a conversation with an archaeologist about their own work? Nearly all the research integrating textual and material data has been done, until very recently, by biblical scholars knowledgeable about archaeology rather than archaeologists knowledgeable about biblical exegesis. The work of history writing will of necessity become less an individual effort and more a collaborative venture.

10

A Bibliographical Review

The volume of recent writing on the history of ancient Israel and Judah is immense and in the last two or three decades there has been intense discussion of all manner of issues. Here is offered a selection of different kinds of published resources, which is intended to illustrate the range of writing rather than a recommendation of the best or most important reading (which is always a matter of opinion).

Approaches to history writing

Two recent reviews of modern historiography on 'ancient Israel' are worth noting: Moore and Kelle (2012) cover both the major contested periods in current historiography and the range of methods deployed, from the mid-twentieth century; they seem particularly designed to assist students from a conservative background (that is, more inclined or educated to view biblical historicity positively), but they do not themselves adopt a conservative view on the subject. Banks (2006) explores the way in which philosophies of history have influenced histories of 'ancient Israel', covering nineteenth-century Germany (Wellhausen in particular), the mid-twentieth century debate centred on the diverging approach of Noth and Bright, and the contemporary debate, in which Thompson figures largely. Brettler (1995) contains helpful sections on the philosophy of history writing too, but his main objective is to explore the many literary devices used in the biblical narratives, such as typology,

interpretation of other texts and rhetoric, which make it difficult
for the exegete who wants to make historical reconstruction. He
stresses how uncertain we must be about the relationship of such
literary creations with the facts of the past. But unlike Thompson
recent work (see below) he prefers to remain with ambiguity over
such a relationship.

Keith Whitelam (1996) has criticized the entire enterprise of
'History of Ancient Israel' as privileging the place of Israel within
the history of Palestine and ignoring the claims of other inhabitants of the region, past and present; he has also (1996) offered
an alternative vision of Iron Age Palestine within a *longue durée*
perspective. Although these two books (and especially the first)
have come in for some heavy criticism, this criticism in many cases
makes his point, which is to show that history writing is not free
from political ideology, especially contemporary Middle Eastern
politics: this is an important lesson to bear in mind, and many of
his detractors seem as clear-sighted regarding Whitelam's as they
are short-sighted regarding their own.

On the identity of 'ancient Israel'

A starting point for recent discussion on this is Davies (1992) with
elaboration in Davies (2007). Though the earlier book was also
greeted with some vigorous protest, its analysis and its questions
seem to have become more sympathetically viewed and even
supported. In fact, the book was not intended as a 'minimalist
manifesto' as it has been called, but a statement of what was seen
as a dilemma in historical research and a suggestion for a way
out of that dilemma – the dilemma chiefly being that the biblical
Israels could not be the object of archaeological research because
they were not sufficiently historical, and that the 'ancient Israel' of
most historical treatments merged the two without discrimination.
The later book tries to explain how the various biblical 'Israels'
came about, especially by the inclusion of Judah in a new Israelite
'people'. Other excellent books that start from these distinctions are by Kratz (2012), bringing a German perspective to the
relationship between 'biblical' and 'historical' Israel in terms of
the distinction between 'Israelite religion' and 'Judaism', and by
Fleming (2012) who builds on the plausible suggestion that the

Pentateuchal material is substantially Israelite, not Judahite, and explores aspects of early 'Israelite' identity in that material as well as the implications of a polemical Judahite scripture.

Histories of 'ancient Israel' (including ancient Judaism)

The purely narrative style of history writing disappeared with John Bright, and all histories now talk rather *about* a narrative. The inclusion of the prophets in such a narrative has also (since Bright) become unusual, perhaps for two reasons: a tendency not to fuse religious and political history in the manner that the biblical stories do, and also a recognition of difficulties in assigning the material in the prophetic books securely to the named prophet (Jeremiah being the major example). The role of archaeological evidence now plays a more prominent and challenging role in historical reconstruction. Thompson's *Early History of the Israelite People* (1992) provides an excellent example of the new kind of history writing from an essentially archaeological-anthropological perspective, including a study of the regional ecology, ethnology, geography, and, rather than co-opt the biblical narrative into the historical reconstruction, Thompson attempts to explain the 'biblical tradition' as a phenomenon in itself. His is essentially a history of Palestine, as the work of Ahlström explicitly titles itself (1993). Ahlström employs a more straightforward chronological structure, and clearly attempts not to prioritize the Iron Age, so placing 'Israel' centre-stage, though because of the volume of the biblical source-material this aim is somewhat frustrated. Both books both make the point that the history of Israel and Judah cannot be told except as part of a fuller history of the region, which must also stretch beyond the rise of the kingdoms of Israel and Judah and even before the Iron Age, thus breaking away from the notion that somehow 'Israel' breaks dramatically into regional history rather than being just a part of it. This way of writing history (with 'Palestine' replaced by 'Canaan') is also exemplified in Noll ([2001] 2013), designed and written for the student, and, as nowadays every history on this topic needs to be, updated. It opens with a long discussion of history writing, followed by a review of pre-Iron Age history before, inevitably, following largely the fate of Israel and Judah and the two provinces. Noll covers almost every aspect of history writing that a student needs to encounter, including the question of religion in Canaan and the 'invention of the Bible'.

The successive editions of Soggin's *Introduction* (1984, 1993, 1999), have been fully updated, so that while, for example, the original edition reads 'Israel' the second reads 'Israel and Judah'. Soggin accurately reflects the ongoing shift towards a more 'minimalist' presentation and offers a readable and reliable book. The first part, entitled 'Introductory Problems' covers the country, the question of 'historiography', then the 'empire' of David and Solomon. Part Two then addresses 'The Traditions about the Origins of the People' (the content of Genesis–Judges), followed by the 'Divided Kingdoms', where historical reconstructed proper begins. Part Four covers the successive empires 'of East and West', and the latest edition has appendices (by D. Conrad and H. Tadmor respectively) on the archaeology of Palestine in the light of the Israelite settlement, and on First Temple chronology. Likewise updated is the more conventional *History of Ancient Israel and Judah* by Miller and Hayes ([1986] 2006; not to be confused with Hayes and Miller 1997, which is a multi-authored book). The second edition, like the first, adheres more closely to the biblical paradigm and maintains its cautious balance regarding historicity, reflecting but not fully endorsing the more sceptical shift in scholarly opinion evidenced by most of the other books mentioned here.

An original approach to the problem of integrating the biblical historiography with a modern critical one has been adopted by Mario Liverani (2005). He divides his account into a 'normal history', starting in the Late Bronze Age and ending with the Neo-Babylonian empire, and a 'constructed history'. The first comprises a straightforward description of the rise of a 'new society' kingdoms in central Palestine in the Iron Age, and the impact of the empires of Assyrian and Babylonia. An 'Intermezzo' sketches the three stages on which Judahite-Jewish history then proceeds: the 'axial age', with its religious, scientific and philosophical innovations across the civilized world, the diasporas that formed in the wake of imperial deportation, and the concomitant economic depression and depopulation in peripheral areas such as Judah. In his 'Invented History' he then describes the 'patriarchal' invention in terms of negotiation between 'returnees' and 'remainees' in Judah; the conquest invention as between 'returnees' and aliens, and the judges era as a reflection of the absence of native monarchy. The 'united monarchy' reflects a 'royal option' for the future and the Solomonic temple a 'priestly option', while the Law develops as a project of self-identification. As a Near Eastern historian and archaeologist, Liverani brings a wider regional outlook to the topic, as well as a reflection, in his Epilogue on the significance of the historian's own cultural context. Liverani's approach has much in common with Thompson's, but differs significantly in its direct linkage of historical fictions with specific aspects of the social realities of post-monarchic life in Judah. Such linkages may turn out to be somewhat too simplistic, but nevertheless pointing in the right direction for an understanding of how such fictions (or substantially fictions) are generated.

In a more recent book Thompson (1999) has spelled out his quite different view of the relationship between history and the biblical stories, largely rejecting the possibility of any historical correlation of the kind proposed by Liverani. Thompson finds biblical storytelling to demonstrate the reworking of a repertoire of conventional themes and plots in different guises – a diagnosis he also applies to the New Testament gospels. Underlying this approach is a long-standing interest in folklore, which brings a different perspective to the understanding of storytelling than that adopted by the approach exemplified by New Historicism.

No reader of current histories can ignore the enormous output of Lester Grabbe (1996, 2000, 2004–6, 2007, 2010, 2012), whose publications on both Israel and Judah and on Judaism generally follow the format of providing a thorough and systematic presentation of every issue, dealing with primary and secondary sources and suggesting what the historical reality is likely to have been. Grabbe does not offer any scheme for the relationship between history and the generation of stories about the past (like Liverani) nor the character of biblical narratives about the past (like Brettler); rather, his approach to the use of biblical sources is to take each case on its merits, his gaze directed to 'what happened' rather than to how the narratives were generated. In some respects, this approach may be viewed as old-fashioned, but no account of the relationship between a social context and the production of stories is possible without establishing the contours of that context as fully as possible. Grabbe is very methodical in systematically reviewing the primary, then secondary literature and then discussing the problems and then synthesizing. Grabbe does not attempt a traditional narrative but his approach strongly implies that there is one, which we can discern, where that is possible, by rigorous examination of sources. As for his contribution to other methodologies, that is abundant in his edited books.

The European seminar in historical methodology

These seminars, all subsequently published in a series, were led and later edited by Lester Grabbe. Most of the seminars were devoted to specific historical issues, whose treatments by the participants were intended to illustrate the application of methodologies and approaches to a common issue. Although the range of participants throughout the series is reasonably large, there is a core of individual scholars each representing a consistent approach to successive topics. If the group overall is somewhat unrepresentative, even somewhat 'minimalist', then it at least represents most of those interested in historical methodology. No voices are heard defending the substantial historicity of all biblical narratives of the past, but such a view is increasingly marginal, and in any event it does not entail much of a method other than rationalization of the biblical narrative.

Perusing this series is an excellent way to immerse oneself in the data and the interplay of interpretations, and each volume has the editor's summary of every contribution. The first volume deals with the fundamental question of whether and how a history can be written, and the last contains a set of reflections on the whole course of the seminar, along with reviews of histories of Israel and related works by other scholars, in some cases with authorial responses to the reviews, where voices outside the seminar can be heard.

To give an idea of the range of topics covered, here is a full list of the volume titles:

1   *Can a 'History of Israel' Be Written?* (1997).

2   *Leading Captivity Captive: 'The Exile' as History and Ideology* (1998).

3   *Did Moses Speak Attic? Jewish Historiography and Scripture in the Hellenistic Period* (2000).

4   *Like a Bird in a Cage: The Invasion of Sennacherib in 701 BCE* (2002).

5   *Good Kings and Bad Kings: The Kingdom of Judah in the Seventh Century BCE* (2005).

6   *Ahab Agonistes: The Rise and Fall of the Omri Dynasty* (2007).

7/1 *Israel in Transition: From Late Bronze II to Iron IIA (c. 1250–850 BCE: The Archaeology)* (2007).

7/2 *Israel in Transition: From Late Bronze II to Iron IIA (c. 1250–850 BCE: The Texts)* (2008).

8   *Enquire of the Former Age: Ancient Historiography and Writing the History of Israel* (2011).

The social world of biblical antiquity and Second Temple studies

These two series were the outcome of two successive conference programmes (their overall contribution was discussed above in Chapter 8). The first generated a set of monographs and one essay collection, while the second series consisted of essay contributed to the meetings of the group. Although the discussions in each series have advances since, the volumes were ground-breaking and illustrate very well how biblical texts, archaeology and social-science modelling can be brought together in a critical historiography.

The full list of titles in the original SWBA series (a second, not connected to the SBL programme, is still current) is as follows:

1   *Monotheism and the Prophetic Minority: An Essay in Biblical History and Sociology* (Lang 1983).

2   *Palestine in Transition: The Emergence of Ancient Israel* (Freedman and Graf 1983).

3   *The Highlands of Canaan: Agricultural Life in the Early Iron Age* (Hopkins 1985).

4   *The Formation of the State in Ancient Israel: A Survey of Models and Theories* (Frick 1985).

5   *The Emergence of Early Israel in Historical Perspective* (Coote and Whitelam 1987).

6   *The Early Biblical Community in Transjordan* (Boling 1988).

7   *David's Social Drama: A Hologram of Israel's Early Iron Age* (Flanagan 1988).

8   *The Forging of Israel: Iron Technology, Symbolism, and Tradition in Ancient Society* (McNutt 1990).

9   *Scribes and Schools in Monarchic Judah: A socio-Archaeological Approach* (Jamieson-Drake 1991).

The volumes of *Second Temple Studies* I–IV appeared between 1991 and 2014 (Davies 1991; Eskenazi and Richards 1994; Davies and Halligan 2002; Hunt 2014).

Judah and the Judeans

The books bearing this title also form a series concentrating on the province of Judah. They are not, either, the result of collaboration or the proceedings of a seminar or conference, but like the previously mentioned series, they share many of the same editors and contributors. They are devoted to the Neo-Babylonian period (Lipschits and Blenkinsopp 2003), the Persian period (Lipschits and Oeming 2006), the fourth century BCE (Knoppers and Albertz 2007), and the Achaemenid period (the early part of the Persian period, and dealing with identity formation; Lipschits, Knoppers and Oeming 2011).

To these can be added three important books on the crucial era between the destruction and revival of Jerusalem (586 BCE – c. 440 BCE): *The Fall and Rise of Jerusalem: Judah under Babylonian Rule* (Lipschits 2005); *The Origins of the 'Second Temple': Persian Imperial Policy and the Rebuilding of Jerusalem* (Edelman 2005) and Faust, *Judah in the Neo-Babylonian Period: The Archaeology of Desolation* (2012b). Both Lipschits and Edelman demonstrate a mastery of both text and archaeology and combine the two effectively in their arguments. Faust's is an archaeological reconstruction, aimed at refuting the view that Judah was not severely devastated after the deportations of 596 and 586. The contours of the fifth century in particular have now become much denser but also more disputed since the application of the results of archaeological surveys demonstrating an interesting contrast between the territory around Jerusalem and the Benjaminite land in the north of the province. No longer can the narratives of Ezra–Nehemiah be more or less trusted to provide an accurate portrait. In general, while the extent of depopulation and the level of economic life in Judah after 586 BCE are still debated, there is general agreement that no single 'return' took place. On the fourth century too little is still known, but a useful collection of essays is in Grabbe and Lipschits 2001.

Archaeology, chronology and history

Two helpful collections of essays introduce and discuss the archaeology of society and the use of radiocarbon dating. The first of these (Levy 1998) offers, first, a set of programmatic essays on approaches to the past, which are followed by sections on the Palaeolithic, then Neolithic, Ages. The last three sections cover the Late Bronze Age–Iron Age transition, then the Iron II–early Roman period, and finally the rise of Christianity and Islam. Here is the fullest account in a single volume of an archaeologically conceived history of human society in Palestine over several millennia, demonstrating the principles of a social-science or anthropological *longue durée* conception of history writing. The virtue of this book is also its drawback. It does not engage with the biblical history, which, from the point of view of its method and philosophy, is entirely correct, even refreshing. This omission, on the other hand, leaves out of account important evidence of the intellectual development of the society of Judah, including the formation of collective memories and strategies of self-identity. This evidence, of course, serves Judah only, and its inclusion would have the effect of assigning more prominence to a rather small society (at least until the second century BCE and after 135 CE). A book such as this, however, reminds us that there is no such thing as 'the history' and no single story of the past. What we wish to narrate depends on our prejudices and assumptions: an important lesson.

The volume on radiocarbon dating (Levy and Higham 2005), is rather less well organized, being the proceedings of a conference. But a good deal of its content addresses the crucial transition from Iron I–II, which entails the issue of the historicity of the Davidic 'empire' or at least a kingdom embracing Judah and Samaria together. Four opening chapters include contributions from the leading protagonists of the 'high' and 'low' chronologies, Mazar and Finkelstein, and the remaining chapters, divided between 'Some Methodological Issues', 'Around the Eastern Mediterranean in the Iron Age', Jordan in the Iron Age, 'Israel in the Iron Age, 'Historical Considerations' and a 'Conclusion'. To potential historians of 'ancient Israel' who will require some familiarity with what is beginning to replace pottery typology with more absolute (or relatively absolute) chronological measurement, this is valuable; and also for demonstrating that even with such exact science, there can remain uncertainty in the conclusions drawn.

A fuller account of the implications and reasoning behind the 'high' and 'low' chronologies can be found in Finkelstein and Mazar (2007) the record of a debate between Finkelstein and Mazar in five parts, to each of which Brian Schmidt has provided assessments. The parts deal with 'Archaeology and the Quest for Historical Israel in the Hebrew Bible', 'Using Archaeology to Assess the Bible's Traditions about "the Earliest Times"', 'The Historical Origins of Collective Israel', 'The Tenth Century: the New Litmus Test for the Bible's Historical Relevance', 'On More Secure Ground? The Kingdoms of Israel and Judah in the Iron II Period', and 'So What? Implications for Scholars and Communities'. This debate therefore covers not only the archaeological evidence and arguments but the implications of these for our understanding of the biblical stories. While the two archaeologists disagree on their assessment of some of the evidence, they converge on Iron II and are in almost total agreement about the proper understanding of the biblical narratives, demonstrating effectively how much the relationship between archaeology and Bible has changed but how much it is no longer a matter of conflict. Archaeology no longer seeks to support the Bible, but to understand properly how and why it engages with the past.

Literary stratigraphy

Two books have been published by Finkelstein and Silberman (2001, 2006), which offer an archaeologically based approach to the biblical narrative, which reveals a settlement in the highlands in Iron I (1250–1050) and the establishment of the Omride kingdom in Samaria as the first 'kingdom of Israel' in the tenth century. The account continues with the period of Assyrian domination, the end of the kingdoms and the establishment of the provinces, in each of which the development of the biblical stories is mapped out. For a readable account of the archaeological history of Israel and Judah this is hard to beat. But they do not merely rewrite the history of Israelite origins, but also assign the various elements of the biblical narrative to their periods of composition.

Their second book on David and Solomon builds on the general picture of archaeological history and literary development estab-lished in the first (the table on pp. 26–31 is especially helpful, aligning successive periods of history with the growing stories of these two kings, the archaeological evidence of the period and the biblical material emanating from it.) According to this table, stories of David as a bandit operating in the lowlands emerge from the tenth century, as do stories of Saul as leader of a small tribal confederacy. The David stories then become elaborated during the life of the Judahite kingdom, becoming written down, combined with the Solomonic tradition and with Israelite traditions in the late eighth century under Hezekiah, and reaching their definitive written form in the first edition of the 'Deuteronomistic History' under Josiah (late seventh century), with more elaboration by the writers of Chronicles in the sixth to fourth centuries.

The correlation of archaeological data with critically recon-structed biblical literature sets an excellent example to historians. The outcome is a kind of literary stratigraphy, with each level identified by archaeological clues. Nevertheless, the reader needs to be cautious about some of the major assumptions, particu-larly relating to Hezekiah and Josiah. Finkelstein and Silberman (Finkelstein has developed this idea in several articles) believe that under Hezekiah, refugees from Samaria after its destruction fled to Judah, swelling the population of Jerusalem and creating a mixed Israelite-Judahite population that combined the traditions of both kingdoms, creating the joint 'Israel' depicted in Genesis–Judges. This is only an interpretation of the evidence that Jerusalem grew rapidly at the end of the eighth century, for which other, perhaps better explanations can be given, such as the flight of Judahite refugees during Sennacherib's invasion of 701, consolidated by Manasseh's prosperous reign as Judah flourished under Assyrian economic exploitation of the region. As for the reign of Josiah, to which the stories of Joshua's conquests are assigned, along with the book of Deuteronomy, there is actually no evidence for this king other than the Bible, which does not state that he wished to annex Samaria. Such a policy is premised on the existence of a power vacuum following the withdrawal of Assyrian power from Palestine. But the Egyptians quickly filled that vacuum. (In any case, the conquest stories of Joshua mostly cover the territory of Benjamin, which was probably already part of Judah under Josiah!) The story of the finding of a law book (Deuteronomy) during Josiah's reign has long been widely accepted as historically reliable, but is now increasingly questioned. The reconstruction thus entails speculation and some questionable argumentation.

Finally, while the books allow for further consolidation of the narratives in the fifth and fourth centuries, Finkelstein has subsequently changed his mind (see Chapter 9) about any literary activity between the time of Josiah and the second century BCE. But these criticisms do not disparage either the effort or the method, which offers an alternative to theories (such as Liverani's) that find a more plausible setting for the bulk of Judah's creation of its past in the post-monarchic era. Indeed, the debate continues between those who wish to assign the essence of the biblical history to the monarchic era and those who wish to place it afterwards. A crucial decision in determining the answer, of course, is the adoption of an Israelite identity within Judah, though it will always be impossible to prove that there were no written accounts of Israel's and Judah's past in the time of their monarchs, unique as such accounts would be.

Keeping up: Journals

The rate and the manner of scholarly communication that has taken place in the last decade has made life both easier and more difficult for the student and scholar. Not so long ago, a handful of books in a generation would suffice, bringing together the published work of a decade or so. Nowadays much more information is available, and it appears at a rate too rapid to allow any major book to avoid obsolescence for long.

As far as biblical exegesis is concerned, there exists at present a wide spectrum of methods and conclusions, hardly any of them carrying a high degree of certainty. Here the burden on the historian lies rather with the need to be aware of the nature of historical research in general, especially on ways in which texts are interrogated for historical information. Like nearly every of the humanities, History is now an interdisciplinary enterprise, and one increasingly aligning itself with the social sciences. But keeping up is a matter of breadth and sustained curiosity rather than a constant search for the latest development. There is no journal specifically devoted to the history of ancient Israel.

With archaeology, the situation is different. To maintain a respectable degree of knowledge it is necessary to keep track of the new data emerging regularly from excavation, survey and laboratory analysis. The quality of the data is also variable. The archaeology of 'ancient Israel' is still embroiled in ideological struggles and with the popular imagination. The sources of information range from highly readable, unreliable and sensational to highly unreadable, technical and useful. Among more popular journals are *Near Eastern Archaeology* and *Biblical Archaeologist*, the former sober, the latter focused more on the Bible and always attracted to the sensational. Very helpful articles can be found alongside highly opinionated ones. Among academic journals, *Tel Aviv* is where most of the work of Tel Aviv's Institute of Archaeology appears; *Israel Exploration Journal* is also an important resource. *Levant* and *Palestine Exploration Quarterly* often include important articles on ancient Israel and Judah.

The internet now offers access to a range of resources, including published articles, lectures and essays, but above all to sites created by and for interest groups with no serious credentials. Surfing websites is good training for the historian, obliging the researcher to ask where the information is coming from, where the evidence is, what are the ideological biases in the presentation, what is the implied audience, and so on. For that reason, would-be historians are encouraged to confront the torrents of misinformation bad history, and unjustified polemic to be found. For, in the end, of the historian can never affirm any historical account as true to the events, it is equally important to identity and condemn what is clearly untrue.

NOTES

What is History?

1   There are any number of books on the theory of history, but especially recommended are the following two: Appleby, Hunt and Jacobs (1994) and Fulbrook (2002), both of which cover in a clear and balanced way most of the aspects of history writing addressed in this *Guide*, but especially in this chapter. Readers of an adventurous political disposition will also enjoy Guldi and Armitage (2014), who, although they do not deal with our period of history, offer a number of relevant challenges to it.

2   In Scotland a verdict of 'not proven' can be given, which leaves the defendant in an awkward position. Such a verdict would have to be given to much of the Bible. But whatever the verdict, it is usually valid on a majority vote, meaning that forensic truth is a democratic principle.

3   Statistics, for example, can establish all kinds of facts, for example, facts about life expectancy, according to class, region and occupation. In the case of 'ancient Israel' archaeological surveys generate very useful facts of this kind.

4   There has been a recent fashion for producing 'what-if?', virtual or alternative histories (for a set of biblical examples, see Exum (ed.) (2000)), taking as a premise that events took another path and trying to reconstruct what might have ensued. Apart from the obvious connection with quantum theory, such exercises are also very useful in reflecting on how we understand historical processes.

Biblical Historiography

1   The Samaritan reading is supported by a fragment of Deuteronomy from Qumran that is not at the time of writing formally published:

see http://www.foundationjudaismchristianorigins.org/ftp/pages/
dead-sea-scrolls/unpub/DSS-deuteronomy.pdf

2   Two kings named Artaxerxes ruled in the fifth to fourth centuries
BCE: Artaxerxes I from 465 to 424 and II from 436 to 358.
Suggestions have been made, in order to avoid placing both Ezra
and Nehemiah too closely together, that Ezra was commissioned by
Artaxerxes II. But this possibility has now been largely abandoned.

3   In foretelling the fate of Abraham's descendants, Yahweh says in
Genesis 15.13 that they will be oppressed in a foreign land for 400
years, while in v. 16, it is predicted that they will return to the land
'in the fourth generation'. A generation is calculated by the age of
the parent when the child is born. The figure of 430 years is given
in Exodus 12.40 for the Israelites' stay in Egypt, and the genealogy
in Exodus 6.14–25 provides four generations from Levi to Moses.
Contradiction is avoided only if the average age of the father when
his first son was born was over 100. This fits the pre-Flood lifespans,
but Moses was 120 when he died (Deut. 34.7), his father Amram
137 (Exod. 6.20) and Amram's father Kohath 123 (Exod. 6.18).

4   On this reconstruction, at any rate, we would expect the Samaritan
Pentateuch to differ, since its chronology will obviously not feature
the Jerusalem temple, and indeed the system can be interpreted to
reflect a calculation of the foundation of the Gerizim Temple by
Phinehas in 2800 AM (*Anno Mundi*). The Septuagint chronologies,
which provide longer periods for the lives of the pre-Abrahamic
figures, are less transparent, but may presuppose a total of 5,000.

Ancient Israel(s) in the Iron Age

1   The reference to *az-ri-a-u* ^matia-u-da-a is seen by a minority of
scholars as a reference to Azariah of Judah; the majority, however,
identify the state in question as *Y'di* (Yaudi), mentioned in a Hittite
inscription from Zinjirli inscription and located in northern Syria.

The 'New Israels':
The Post-monarchic Era

1   There is a mediaeval Samaritan Book of Joshua in Arabic.

2   It is true that C. C. Torrey dismissed the whole account of exile and

restoration as unhistorical, but his views were mostly either ignored or dismissed. For recent dismantling of their historicity see Davies 1995, Grabbe 1998 (on Ezra) and Wright 2004 (on Nehemiah).

3   There is a similar profile in the *Damascus Document* from Qumran, where an 'Interpreter of the Law' (unnamed) is remembered as the founder of the new Israel after the destruction of the first Israel.

4   The connection between Abraham and Ur (Gen. 11.28–31) is a geographical connection that may have two reasons: narratively, as illustrating the spread of humanity from Babel, focusing on this particular family; or as extending Abraham's patrimony to the Mesopotamian diasporas of Judah and Samaria.

Archaeology

1   The final quotation here is from Hobsbawm in Hobsbawm and Ranger 1983: 14.

Sociological Approaches to History

1   The term 'Thick Description' itself was coined by the philosopher Gilbert Ryle, and used in his lecture 'The Thinking of Thoughts: What is "Le Penseur" Doing?' reprinted in *Collected Papers*, 2, London: Hutchinson (1971), 480–96.

BIBLIOGRAPHY

Abu el-Haj, N. (2001), *Facts on the Ground: Archaeological Practice and Territorial Self-Fashioning in Israeli Society*, Chicago, IL: University of Chicago Press.

Ahn, J. (2010), *Exile as Forced Migrations: A Sociological, Literary, and Theological Approach on the Displacement and Resettlement of the Southern Kingdom of Judah*, Berlin: De Gruyter.

Ahlström, G. (1993), *The History of Ancient Palestine*, Sheffield: JSOT Press.

Albright, W. F. (1942), *From the Stone Age to Christianity: Monotheism and the Historical Process*, Baltimore, MD: Johns Hopkins University Press.

Appleby, J., L. Hunt and M. Jacobs (1994), *Telling the Truth about History*, London: W. W. Norton.

Assmann, J. ([1992] 2005), *Das kulturelle Gedächtnis. Schrift, Erinnerung und politische Identität in frühen Hochkulturen*, 6th edn, Munich: Beck.

Assmann, J. (2005), *Religion and Cultural Memory*, Redwood City, CA: Stanford University Press.

Athas, G. (2003), *The Tel Dan Inscription: A Reappraisal and a New Interpretation*, Sheffield: Sheffield Academic Press.

Auld, A. G. (1994), *Kings without Privilege: David and Moses in the Story of the Bible's Kings*, Edinburgh: T&T Clark.

—(2011), *First and Second Samuel: A Commentary*, London: SCM Press and Louisville, KY: Westminster John Knox Press.

Banks, D. (2006), *Writing the History of Israel*, London: T&T Clark.

Barstad, H. (2002), 'Is the Hebrew Bible a Hellenistic Book? Or: Niels Peter Lemche, Herodotus, and the Persians', *Transeuphratène*, 23: 129–51.

Bartlett, F. C. (1932), *Remembering: A Study in Experimental and Social Psychology*, Cambridge: Cambridge University Press.

Baumgarten, A. I. (1997), *The Flourishing of Jewish Sects in the Maccabean Era: An Interpretation*, Leiden: Brill.

Beattie, D. R. G. and P. R. Davies (2011), 'What Does "Hebrew" Mean?', *JSS*, 56: 71–83.

Becking, B. (1992), *The Fall of Samaria: An Historical and Archaeological Study*, Leiden: Brill.

Blenkinsopp, J. (1991), 'Temple and Society in Achaemenid Judah', in P. R. Davies (ed.), *Second Temple Studies I: Persian Period*, 163–74, Sheffield: JSOT Press.

—(2006), *Opening the Sealed Book: Interpretations of the Book of Isaiah in Late Antiquity*, Winona Lake, IN: Eerdmans.

Boling, R. G. (1988), *The Early Biblical Community in Transjordan*, Sheffield: Almond Press.

Braudel, F. (1975), *The Mediterranean and the Mediterranean World in the Age of Philip II*, London: Fontana.

Brettler, M. Z. (1995), *The Creation of History in Ancient Israel*, London: Routledge.

Bright, J. (1960), *A History of Israel*, Philadelphia, PA: Westminster Press; 4th edn, London: SCM Press, 2000.

Burke, P. (2013), *The French Historical Revolution: Annales School 1929-1989*, Hoboken, NJ: Wiley.

Chalcraft, D. (ed.) (2008), *Sectarianism in Early Judaism: Sociological Advances*, London: Equinox, 2008.

Cline, E. H. (2009), *Biblical Archaeology: A Very Short Introduction*, Oxford: Oxford University Press.

Coote, R. and K. W. Whitelam (1987), *The Emergence of Early Israel in Historical Perspective*, Sheffield: Almond Press.

Cross, F. M. (1973), *Canaanite Myth and Hebrew Epic: Essays in the History of the Religion of Israel*, Cambridge, MA: Harvard University Press.

Davies, P. R. (ed.) (1991), *Second Temple Studies I: Persian Period*, Sheffield: JSOT Press.

—(1992), *In Search of Ancient Israel*, Sheffield: Sheffield Academic Press.

—(1995), 'Scenes from the Early History of Judaism', in D. V. Edelman (ed.), *The Triumph of Elohim* (Contributions to Biblical Exegesis and Theology), 145–82, Kampen: Kok Pharos.

—(ed.) (1996), 'The Audiences of Prophetic Scrolls: Some Suggestions', in S. Breck Reid (ed.), *Prophets and Paradigms: Essays in Honor of Gene M. Tucker*, 48–62, Sheffield: Sheffield Academic Press.

—(1998), *Scribes and Schools: The Canonization of the Hebrew Scriptures*, Louisville, KY: Westminster John Knox Press.

—(2007), *The Origins of Biblical Israel*, London: T&T Clark.

—(2008), *Memories of Ancient Israel: An Introduction to Biblical History*, Louisville, KY: Westminster John Knox Press.

—(2010), 'The Beginnings of the Kingdom of Judah', in L. L. Grabbe (ed.), *Israel in Transition 2*, 54–61, London: T&T Clark.

—(2013), 'Land of Israel', in A. H. Cadwallader (ed.), *Where the Wild*

Ox Roams: Biblical Essays in Honour of Norman C. Habel, 32–41, Sheffield: Sheffield Phoenix Press.

Davies, P. R. and J. M. Halligan (eds) (2002), *Second Temple Studies III: Studies in Politics, Class and Material Culture*, Sheffield: Sheffield Academic Press.

Davis, T. W. (2004), *Shifting Sands: The Rise and Fall of Biblical Archaeology*, New York: Oxford University Press.

Edelman, D. (2001), 'Did Saulide-Davidic Rivalry Resurface in Early Persian Yehud?', in M. P. Graham and A. Dearman (eds), *The Land that I Will Show You: Essays in the History and Archaeology of the Ancient Near East in Honor of J. Maxwell Miller*, 70–92, Sheffield: Sheffield Academic Press.

—(2005), *The Origins of the 'Second Temple': Persian Imperial Policy and the Rebuilding of Jerusalem*, London: Equinox.

Eisenstadt, S. N. (1963), *The Political Systems of Empires*, London: Free Press of Glencoe.

Eskenazi, T. and K. Richards (eds) (1994), *Second Temple Studies II: Temple and Community in the Persian Period*, Sheffield: JSOT Press.

Exum, J. C. (ed.) (2000), *Virtual History and the Bible*, Leiden: Brill.

Faust, A. (2012a), *The Archaeology of Israelite Society in Iron Age II*, Winona Lake, IN: Eisenbrauns.

—(2012b), *Judah in the Neo-Babylonian Period: The Archaeology of Desolation*, Atlanta, GA: Society of Biblical Literature.

Finkelstein, I. (1988), *The Archaeology of the Israelite Settlement*, Jerusalem: Israel Exploration Society.

—(2006a), 'The Last Labayu: King Saul and the Expansion of the First North Israelite Territorial Entity', in Y. Amit, E. Ben Zvi, I. Finkelstein and O. Lipschits (eds), *Essays on Ancient Israel in Its Near Eastern Context: A Tribute to Nadav Na'aman*, 171–7, Winona Lake, IN: Eisenbrauns.

—(2006b), 'Temple and Dynasty: Hezekiah, the Remaking of Judah and the Rise of the Pan-Israelite Ideology', *JSOT*, 30: 259–85.

—(2007), 'Has King David's Palace in Jerusalem been Found?', *Tel Aviv*, 34: 142–62.

—(2008), 'Jerusalem in the Persian (and Early Hellenistic) Period and the Wall of Nehemiah', *JSOT*, 32: 501–20.

—(2009), 'Persian Period Jerusalem and Yehud: A Rejoinder', *JHS*, 9: 2–13.

—(2013), *The Forgotten Kingdom: The Archaeology and History of Northern Israel*, Atlanta, GA: SBL.

Finkelstein, I. and A. Mazar (2007), *The Quest for the Historical Israel*, Leiden: Brill.

Finkelstein, I. and T. Römer (2014a), 'Comments on the Historical

Background of the Abraham Narrative: Between "Realia" and "Exegetica"', *Hebrew Bible and Ancient Israel*, 3: 3–23.

—(2014b), 'Comments on the Historical Background of the Jacob Narrative in Genesis', *ZAW*, 126: 317–38.

Finkelstein, I. and N. A. Silberman (2001), *The Bible Unearthed: Archaeology's New Vision of Ancient Israel and the Origin of Its Sacred Texts*, New York: Free Press.

—(2006), *David and Solomon: In Search of the Bible's Sacred Kings and the Roots of the Western Tradition*, New York: Free Press.

Flanagan, J. W. (1988), *David's Social Drama: A Hologram of Israel's Early Iron Age*, Sheffield: Almond Press.

Fleming, D. E. (2012), *The Legacy of Israel in Judah's Bible: History, Politics, and the Reinscribing of Tradition*, New York: Cambridge University Press.

Foucault, M. (1972), *The Archaeology of Knowledge*, London: Tavistock Publications.

Freedman, D. N. and D. Graf (eds) (1983), *Palestine in Transition: The Emergence of Ancient Israel*, Sheffield: Almond Press.

Frick, F. S. (1985), *The Formation of the State in Ancient Israel: A Survey of Models and Theories*, Sheffield: Almond Press.

Fulbrook, M. (2002), *Historical Theory*, London: Routledge.

Garfinkel, Y. and S. Ganor (2008), 'Tel Qeiyafa: Sha'araym', *JHS*, 8 (article 22).

Geertz, C. (1973), *The Interpretation of Cultures: Selected Essays*, New York: Basic Books.

Gmirkin, R. (2006), *Berossus and Genesis, Manetho and Exodus*, London: T&T Clark.

Gottwald, N. (1979), *The Tribes of Yahweh: A Sociology of the Religion of Liberated Israel, 1250–1050 B.C.E.*, Maryknoll, NY: Orbis Books.

Grabbe, L. L. (1996), *An Introduction to First Century Judaism: Jewish Religion and History in the Second Temple Period*, Edinburgh: T&T Clark.

Grabbe, L. L. (ed.) (1997), *Can a 'History of Israel' Be Written?*, Sheffield: Sheffield Academic Press.

—(1998), *Ezra–Nehemiah*, London: Routledge.

—(ed.) (1998), *Leading Captivity Captive: 'The Exile' as History and Ideology*, Sheffield: Sheffield Academic Press.

—(ed.) (2000), *Judaic Religion in the Second Temple Period: Belief and Practice from the Exile to Yavneh*, London: Routledge.

—(ed.) (2001), *Did Moses Speak Attic? Jewish Historiography and Scripture in the Hellenistic Period*, Sheffield: Sheffield Academic Press.

—(ed.) (2002), *Like a Bird in a Cage: The Invasion of Sennacherib in 701 bce*, Sheffield: Sheffield Academic Press.

—(2004, 2006), *A History of the Jews and Judaism in the Second Temple Period*, 2 vols, London: T&T Clark.

—(ed.) (2005), *Good Kings and Bad Kings: The Kingdom of Judah in the Seventh Century* BCE, London: T&T Clark.

—(2007), *Ancient Israel: What Do We Know and How Do We Know It?*, London: T&T Clark.

—(ed.) (2007), *Ahab Agonistes: The Rise and Fall of the Omri Dynasty*, London: T&T Clark.

—(ed.) (2007), *Israel in Transition: From Late Bronze II to Iron IIA (c. 1250–850 BCE: The Archaeology*, London: T&T Clark.

—(2010), *An Introduction to Second Temple Judaism: History and Religion of the Jews in the Time of Nehemiah, the Maccabees, Hillel and Jesus*, London: T&T Clark.

—(ed.) (2010), *Israel in Transition II: From Late Bronze II to Iron IIA (c. 1250–850 BCE): The Texts*, London: T&T Clark.

—(ed.) (2011), *Enquire of the Former Age: Ancient Historiography and Writing the History of Israel*, London: T&T Clark.

—(2012), *Judaism from Cyrus to Hadrian*, 2 vols, Minneapolis, MN: Fortress Press.

Grabbe, L. L. and O. Lipschits (eds) (2011), *Judah between East and West: The Transition from Persian to Greek Rule (ca. 400–200 BCE)*, London: T&T Clark.

Greenberg, M. (1955), *The Hab/piru*, New Haven, CT: American Oriental Society.

Guldi, J. and D. Armitage (2014), *The History Manifesto*, Cambridge: Cambridge University Press.

Halbwachs, M. ([1925] 1952), *Les cadres sociaux de la mémoire*, Paris: Alcan; English translation, *On Collective Memory*, (ed. and trans.) L. A. Coser, Chicago, IL: University of Chicago Press, 1992 (from the revised edn, 1952).

Halpern, B. (1995), 'Erasing History: The Minimalist Assault on Ancient Israel', *Bible Review*, 11: 26–35, 47.

—(1996), *The First Historians: The Hebrew Bible and History*, University Park, PA: Pennsylvania State University Press.

Hayes J. H. and J. M. Miller (eds) (1977), *Israelite and Judaean History*, London and Philadelphia, PA: SCM/Trinity Press International.

Hens-Piazza, G. (2002), *New Historicism*, Philadelphia, PA: Fortress.

Hobsbawm, E. and T. Ranger (eds) (1983), *The Invention of Tradition*, Cambridge: Cambridge University Press.

Hopkins, D. C. (1985), *The Highlands of Canaan*, Sheffield: Almond Press.

Huizinga, J. (1936), 'A Definition of a Concept of History', in
    R. Klibanski and H. J. Paton (eds), *Philosophy and History*, Oxford:
    Clarendon Press.
Hunt, A. (ed.) (2014), *Second Temple Studies IV: Historiography and
    History*, London: T&T Clark.
Kletter, R. (2005), *Just Past? The Making of Israeli Archaeology*,
    London: Equinox.
Jameson, F. (1981), *The Political Unconscious: Narrative as a Socially
    Symbolic Act*, Ithaca, NY: Cornell University Press.
Jamieson-Drake, D. W. (1991), *Scribes and Schools in Monarchic Judah*,
    Sheffield: Almond Press.
Japhet, S. (1989), *The Ideology of the Book of Chronicles and Its Place
    in Biblical Thought*, Frankfurt: Peter Lang [Hebrew 1977].
Jones, S. (1997), *The Archaeology of Ethnicity*, London: Routledge.
Knauf, E. A. (2010), 'Biblical References to Judean Settlement in Eretz
    Israel (and Beyond) in the Late Persian and Early Hellenistic Periods',
    in P. R. Davies and D. V. Edelman (eds), *The Historian and the
    Bible: Essays in Honour of Lester L. Grabbe*, 175–93, London:
    T&T Clark.
Knoppers, G. and R. Albertz (eds) (2007), *Judah and the Judeans in the
    Fourth Century BCE*, Winona Lake, IN: Eisenbrauns.
Kratz, R. G. (2012), *Historisches und biblisches Israel. Drei Überblicke
    zum alten Testament*, Tübingen: Mohr.
Lang, B. (1983), *Monotheism and the Prophetic Minority: An Essay in
    Biblical History and Sociology*, Sheffield: Almond Press.
Lee, S., C. B. Ramsey and A. Mazar (2013), 'Iron Age Chronology
    in Israel: Results from Modeling with a Trapezoidal Bayesian
    Framework', *Radiocarbon*, 55: 731–40.
Lefebvre, H. (1991), *The Production of Space*, Oxford: Blackwell.
Lemaire, A. (1973), 'Asriel, Šr'l, Israel et l'origine de la confederation
    Israelite', *VT*, 23: 239–43.
—(1994), '"House of David" Restored in Moabite Inscription', *BAR*, 20
    (3): 30–7.
Lemche, N. P. (1976), 'The Greek Amphictyony – Could It Be a
    Prototype for the Israelite Society in the Period of the Judges?', *JSOT*,
    4: 48–59.
—(1986), *Early Israel: Anthropological and Historical Studies on the
    Israelite Society before the Monarchy*, Leiden: Brill.
—(1988), *Ancient Israel: A New History of Israelite Society*, Sheffield:
    Sheffield Academic Press.
—(1993), 'The Bible – A Hellenistic Book?', *SJOT*, 7: 163–93.
—(1995), 'Kings and Clients: On Loyalty between the Ruler and the
    Ruled in 'Ancient' Israel', *Semeia*, 66: 119–32.

Lévi-Strauss, C. (1972), *The Savage Mind*, London: Weidenfeld and Nicolson.

Levy, T. (ed.) ([1995] 1998), *The Archaeology of Society in the Holy Land*, 2nd edn, Leicester: Leicester University Press.

Levy, T. and T. Higham (eds) (2005), *The Bible and Radiocarbon Dating*, London: Equinox.

Lipschits, O. (2005), *The Fall and Rise of Jerusalem: Judah under Babylonian Rule*, Winona Lake, IN: Eisenbrauns.

Lipschits, O. and J. Blenkinsopp (eds) (2003), *Judah and the Judeans in the Neo-Babylonian Period*, Winona Lake, IN: Eisenbrauns.

Lipschits, O., G. Knoppers and M. Oeming (eds) (2011), *Judah and the Judeans in the Achaemenid Period: Negotiating Identity in an International Context*, Winona Lake, IN: Eisenbrauns.

Lipschits, O. and M. Oeming (eds) (2006), *Judah and the Judeans in the Persian Period*, Winona Lake, IN: Eisenbrauns.

Liverani, M. (2005), *Israel's History and the History of Israel*, London: Equinox.

McNutt, P. M. (1990), *The Forging of Israel: Iron Technology, Symbolism, and Tradition in Ancient Society*, Sheffield: JSOT Press.

Marincola, J. (1997), *Authority and Tradition in Ancient Historiography*, Cambridge: Cambridge University Press.

Mazar, E. (2006), 'Did I Find King David's Palace?', *BAR*, 32: 16–27, 70.

Mendels, D. (1992), *The Rise and Fall of Jewish Nationalism: Jewish and Christian Ethnicity in Ancient Palestine*, Grand Rapids, MI: Eerdmans.

—(2004), *Memory in Jewish, Pagan, and Christian Societies of the Graeco-Roman World*, London: T&T Clark.

—(ed.)(2007), *On Memory: An Interdisciplinary Approach*, Oxford: Peter Lang.

Mendenhall, G. E. (1962), 'The Hebrew Conquest of Palestine', *BA*, 25: 66–87.

Miller J. M. and J. H. Hayes ([1986] 2006), *A History of Ancient Israel and Judah*, London: SCM Press.

Moore, M. B. and B. Kelle (2012), *Biblical History and Israel's Past: The Changing Study of the Bible and History*, Grand Rapids, MI: Eerdmans.

Moorey, R. (1981), *Excavation in Palestine*, Guildford: Lutterworth Press.

Na'aman, N. (2008), 'In Search of the Ancient Name of Khirbet Qeiyafa', *JHS*, 8 (article 21).

Nielsen, F. (1997), *The Tragedy in History: Herodotus and the Deuteronomistic History*, Sheffield: Sheffield Academic Press.

Noll, K. ([2001] 2013), *Canaan and Israel in Antiquity*, 2nd edn, London: Continuum/Bloomsbury.

Noth, M. (1958), *The History of Israel*, London: A&C Black.

—(1972), *A History of Pentateuchal Traditions*, Englewood Cliffs, NJ: Prentice-Hall [German 1948].

—(1991), *The Deuteronomistic History*, Sheffield: JSOT Press [German 1943].

Oded, B. (1979), *Mass Deportations and Deportees in the Neo-Assyrian Empire*, Wiesbaden: Reichert.

Rad, G. von (1960), 'History and the Patriarchs', *Expository Times*, 72: 213–16.

Radley, A. (1990), 'A Social Psychological Approach: Artefacts, Memory and Making Sense of the Past', in D. Middleton and D. E. Edwards (eds), *Collective Remembering*, 46–59, London: Sage.

Regev, E. (2007), *Sectarianism in Qumran: A Cross-Cultural Perspective*, Berlin: De Gruyter.

Rendtorff, R. (1990), *The Problem of the Process of Transmission in the Pentateuch*, Sheffield : JSOT Press.

Rogerson, J. W. (2010), *A Theology of the Old Testament: Cultural Memory, Communication and Being Human*, London: SPCK, and Minneapolis, MN: Fortress.

Römer, T. (2007), *The So-called Deuteronomistic History: A Sociological, Historical, and Literary Introduction*, London: T&T Clark.

—(2013), 'Conflicting Models of Identity and the Publication of the Torah in the Persian Period', in R. Albertz and J. Wöhrle (eds), *Between Cooperation and Hostility: Multiple Identities in Ancient Judaism and the Interaction with Foreign Powers*, 33–51, Göttingen: Vandenhoeck & Ruprecht.

Sacks, O. (1986), *The Man Who Mistook His Wife for a Hat*, London: Summit Books.

Schwartz, D. R. (2013), 'Judeans, Jews, and Their Neighbors', in R. Albertz and J. Wöhrle (eds), *Between Cooperation and Hostility: Multiple Identities in Ancient Judaism and the Interaction with Foreign Powers*, 13–31, Göttingen: Vandenhoeck & Ruprecht.

Shavit, Y. (1997), 'Archaeology, Political Culture, and Culture in Israel', in N. A. Silberman and D. B. Small (eds), *The Archaeology of Israel: Constructing the Past, Interpreting the Present*, 48–61, Sheffield, Sheffield Academic Press.

Soggin, J. A. (1984), *Introduction to the History of Israel*, London: SCM Press; 2nd edn, *Introduction to the History of Israel and Judah*, 1993; 3rd edn, 1999.

Soja, E. W. (1971), *The Political Organization of Space*, Washington, DC: Association of American Geographers.

Sparks, K. L. (1998), *Ethnicity and Identity in Ancient Israel: Prolegomena to the Study of Ethnic Sentiments and Their Expression in the Hebrew Bible*, Winona Lake, IN: Eisenbrauns.

Steiner, M. (2003), 'Expanding Borders: The Development of Jerusalem in the Iron Age', in T. L. Thompson (ed.), *Jerusalem in Ancient History and Tradition*, 68–79, London: T&T Clark.

Talmon, S. (1988), *Gesellschaft und Literatur in der Hebräischen Bibel*, 3 vols, Neukirchen: Neukirchener Verlag.

Thompson, T. L. (1974), *The Historicity of the Patriarchal Narratives*, Berlin: De Gruyter.

—(1999), *The Bible in History: How Writers Create a Past*, London: Jonathan Cape.

Thompson, T. L. and P. Wajdebaum (eds) (2014), *The Bible and Hellenism*, Durham: Acumen.

Torrey, C. C. (1910), *Ezra Studies*, Chicago, IL: University of Chicago Press.

Van Seters, J. (1975), *Abraham in History and Tradition*, New Haven, CT: Yale University Press.

—(1983), *In Search of History: Historiography in the Ancient World and the Origins of Biblical History*, New Haven, CT: Yale University Press.

Vaughn, A. G. and A. E. Killebrew (eds) (2003), *Jerusalem in Bible and Archaeology: The First Temple Period*, Atlanta, GA: Society of Biblical Literature.

Veeser, H. A. (ed.) (1989), *The New Historicism*, New York: Routledge.

Younger, K. L. (1998), 'The Deportation of the Israelites', *JBL*, 117: 201–27.

Wajdebaum, P. (2011), *Argonauts of the Desert: Structural Analysis of the Hebrew Bible*, Sheffield: Equinox.

Watts, J. W. (ed.) (2001), *Persia and Torah: The Theory of Imperial Authorization of the Pentateuch*, Atlanta, GA: Society of Biblical Literature.

Wellhausen, J. (1885), *Prolegomena to the History of Ancient Israel*, Edinburgh: A&C Black.

Wesselius, J.-W. (2002), *The Origin of the History of Israel*, Sheffield: Sheffield Academic Press.

de Wette, W. M. L. (1806), *Beiträge zur Einleitung in das Alte Testament*, Halle: Schimmelpfennig.

Whitelam, K. W. (1996), *The Invention of Ancient Israel: The Silencing of Palestinian History*, London: Routledge.

—(2013), *Rhythms of Time: Reconnecting Palestine's Past*, Ben Black Books [electronic publication]. Available online: http://www.rhythmsoftime.com (accessed 10 February 2015).

Williams, R. (1977), *Marxism and Literature*, Oxford: Oxford University
    Press.
Williamson, H. G. M. (1977), *Israel in the Books of Chronicles*,
    Cambridge: Cambridge University Press.
Wright, G. E. (1960), 'Modern Issues in Biblical Studies: History and the
    Patriarchs', *Expository Times* 71: 292–96.
Wright, J. L. (2004), *Rebuilding Identity: The Nehemiah Memoir and Its
    Earliest Readers*, Berlin: De Gruyter.
Yerushalmi, Y. H. (1982), *Zakhor: Jewish History and Jewish Memory*,
    Seattle, WA: University of Washington Press.
Zerubavel, E. (2003), *Time Maps: Collective Memory and the Social
    Shape of the Past*, Chicago, IL: Chicago University Press.
Zerubavel, Y. (2005), *Recovered Roots: Collective Memory and the
    Making of Israeli National Tradition*, Chicago, IL: University of
    Chicago Press.

INDEX OF MODERN
AUTHORS

Abu el-Haj, N. 117, 130
Adorno, T. 122
Ahlström, G. 155
Ahn, J. 135
Albertz, R. 160
Albright, W. F. 5, 65
Alt, A. 5, 6
Althusser R. 122
Appleby, J. 167
Armitage, D. 167
Assmann, J. xii, 128, 130–2
Auld, A. G. 43, 55, 146

Banks, D. 153
Barstad, H. 37
Bartlett, F. C. 128
Baumgarten, A. 135
Benjamin, W. 122
Blenkinsopp, J. 135, 160
Bloch, M. xi, 119
Boling, R. G. 160
Braudel, F. ix, 119
Brettler, M. Z. 153
Bright, J. 5, 8, 9, 153

Cahill, J. 117
Chalcraft 135
Cline, E. 104
Conrad, D. 156
Coote, R. 160

Davies, P.R. 61, 73, 95, 135, 154,
    160, 169

Davis, T. W. 104

Edelman, D. V. 47, 146, 160–1
Eisenstadt, S. N. 134
Eskenazi, T. 160
Exum, J. C. 167

Faust, A. 141, 160–1
Febvre, L. 119
Finkelstein, I. 78, 94, 116–17,
    144, 162–4
Flanagan, J. W. 160
Fleming, D. E. 91, 154
Foucault, M. 121
Freedman, D.N. 159
Frick, F. S. 77, 160

Ganor, S. 69
Garfinkel, Y. 69, 117
Geertz, C. 122–4
Gmirkin, R. 37
Gottwald, N. K. 10, 133–4
Grabbe, L. L. 112, 157–9, 161,
    169
Graf, D. 159
Graf, K. H. 2
Greenberg, M. 98
Guldi, J. 167

Habermas, J. 122
Halbwachs, M. 126, 130
Halligan, J. M. 160
Halpern, B. 12, 28

Hayes, J. H. 93, 156
Hens-Piazza, G. 122
Higham, T. 107, 162
Hobsbawm, E. 130, 169
Hopkins, D. C. 160
Horkheimer, M. 122
Huizinga, J. 29
Hunt, A. 160
Hunt, L. 167

Jacobs, M. 167
Jameson, F. 122
Jamieson-Drake, D. W. 117, 160
Japhet, S 40
Jones, S. 110

Kelle, B. 153
Killebrew, A. 117
Kletter, R. 130
Knauf, E. A. 97
Knoppers, G. 160
Kratz, R. G. 140, 154

Lang, B. 159
Lefebvre, H. 129
Lemaire, A. 71, 76
Lemche, N. P. 37, 135
Lévi-Strauss, C. 121, 131
Levy, T. 107, 161–2
Lipschits, O. 160–1
Liverani, M. 156

McNutt, P. M. 160
Mannheim, K. 122
Marincola, J. 28
Mazar, A. 114, 162
Mazar, E. 69, 117
Mendels, D. 98, 130–1
Mendenhall, G. E. 10
Miller, J.M. 93, 156
Moore, M. Bishop 153
Moorey, P. R. S. 104

Na'aman, N. 117
Nielsen, F. 37
Noll, K. 28, 155
Noth, M. 5, 6, 8, 9, 12, 42–3,
    65–6, 135, 153

Oded, B. 135
Oeming, M. 160

Payne, T. 2
Petrie, W. M. Flinders 104

Rad, G. von 6–7
Radley, A. 126
Ranger, T. 130, 169
Regev, E. 135
Rendtorff, R. 6
Richards, K. 160
Rogerson, J. W. 132
Römer, T. 144
Ryle, G. 124, 169

Sacks, O. 126–7
Schliemann, H. 104
Schwartz, D. 98
Shavit, S. 130
Silberman, N. A. 163–4
Soggin, J. A. 156
Soja, E. 129
Sparks, K. L. 110
Spinoza, B. 2
Steiner, M. 117

Tadmor, H. 156
Talmon, S. 135
Thompson, T. L. 10, 52, 145,
    153, 155, 157
Torrey, C. C. 168

Van Seters, J. 10, 29, 33
Vaughn, A. 117
Voltaire, F.-M. 2

Wajdebaum, P. 37
Watts, J. D. 150
Weber, M. 11
Wellhausen, J. 2, 8, 51, 60, 83,
    96, 140, 153
Wesselius, J.-W. 37
Wette, W. M. L. de 2, 83, 140
Whitelam, K. W. ix, xi, 113, 154,
    160
Williams, R. 121–2

Williamson, H. G. M. 40
Wright, G. E. 7
Wright, J. L. 47, 169

Yadin, Y. 115
Yerushalmi, Y. H. 131

Zerubavel, E. 131
Zerubavel, Y. 131

INDEX OF ANCIENT SOURCES

Non-biblical
Babylonian Chronicle(s) 32–3
Berossus 37
'Black Obelisk' 72

Diodorus 40.3 148

Genesis Apocryphon 54–5

Hecataeus of Abdera 97, 148–9
Hecataeus of Miletus 34–5
Herodotus 35–8

Josephus, *Against Apion* 148

Kurkh Stele 72, 115

Letter of Aristeas 12–14 149

Manetho 37, 97, 148–9
Merneptah Stele 70–1
Mesha inscription 75–6

'Rimah Stele' 72

Sumerian King List 30

Tel Dan inscription 75–6

Zinjirli inscription 168

Biblical
Genesis
5 49
6.1–4 30
9.28–9 49
10–11 56, 59
11.10–26 49
11.28–31 169
12 147
14.13 98
15.13, 16 168
28 84
39–41 98
42 147

Exodus
1–2 98
6.14–25 168
6.18 168
6.20 168
12.40 51, 168
21.2 98

Leviticus
25 51
26.35 51

Numbers
36.21 71

Deuteronomy
12.5, 14 82
18.12 98
26.5–10 7
27.4–5 44
34.7 168

Joshua
15.63 56
17.2 71
18.28 56

Judges
1.8 56
1.21 56
11 38
17–21 145
20.1 81

1 Samuel
3.20 81
5.6 57
13.1 49
17 145
17.54 56

2 Samuel
3.10 81
7 81
9–20 43, 55
17.11 81
24.2, 15 81

1 Kings
1–2 43, 55
4.25 81
6.1 51
8 82
9.15 115
11 82
11.40 116
12 84
25 70, 116

2 Kings
1–8 92
1.17 92
3 75–6
3.1,7 93
8.16 93
10 115
13.10 50
14.1–2 50
14.23 50
15.10 50
16.15–29 50
17 82–4, 90, 150
17.6 100
18 50, 59
18.11 100
23.22 53
25.12 84
25.26 149

1 Chronicles
1–9 43
17.14 71
21.2 81

2 Chronicles
13.22 37
15.9 86
20 41
21 93
24.27 37
30.5 81
31.1, 10–11, 25 85
35.20–1 86
36.21 51
36.22–3 88

Ezra
1–2 46, 89
1–3 51
2.2, 70 46, 89
4.1 89
4.9–10 90
4.24 52

6–7 46–7
6.16 90
7 46
10.9 89

Nehemiah
4.2 90
8–12 47
8 46
8.17 90
12 46
13.3–4 90

Isaiah
36–9 60
40–55 88
40–66 61, 96
45 30
45.1 88

Jeremiah
11.18–12.6 61
15.10–21 61
17.14–18 61
18.18–23 61
20.7–18 61
25.11–12 51
29.10 51
34.9 98
43–4 149
44.1, 15 149
52 60

Daniel
2 49
7–8 34
9 49
9.2 51

Amos
7 60
9 88

Jonah
1.9 98

Zechariah
7.5 51

Apocrypha
4 Ezra 48
2 Maccabees
1 48

New Testament
Matthew
1.17 49

Philippians
3.5 98–9